LEARNING TO SEE

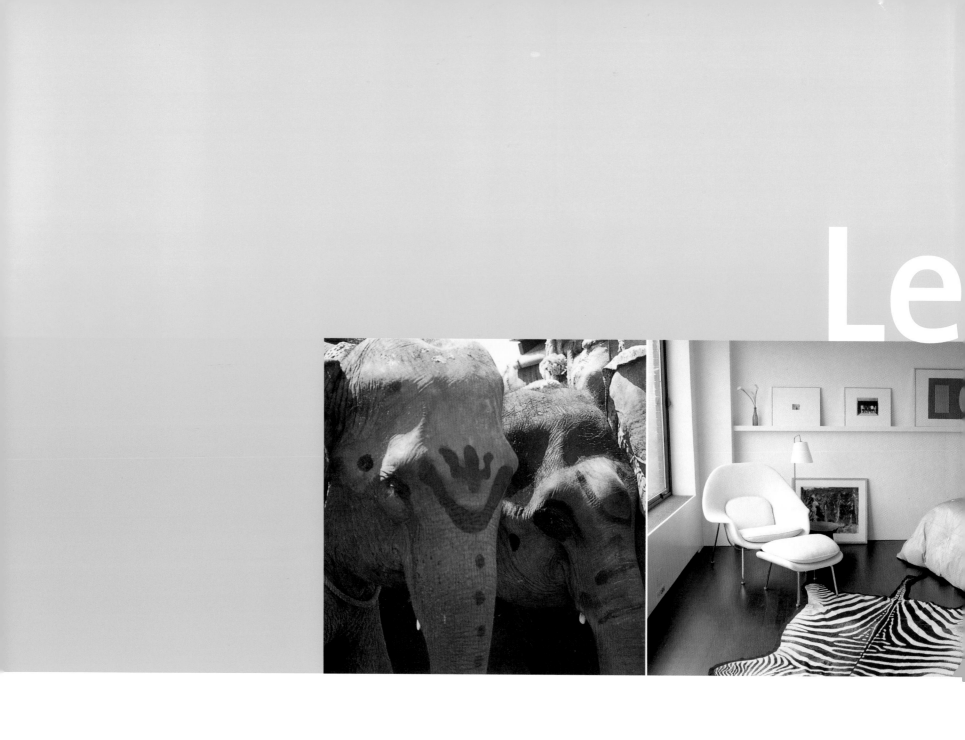

Le

arning to See

Bringing the World
Around You Into Your Home

Words and Photographs by Vicente Wolf

Foreword by Louis Oliver Gropp

Artisan  New York

I PUSHED OPEN THE HEAVY WOODEN DOORS of a six-hundred-year-old temple in Bhutan. For a moment I could see nothing. The fragrance of incense was overpowering. As my eyes gradually adjusted to the dimness, I could make out the blur of painted figures on a wall. An immense statue of Buddha towered in front of me. Hot pink and yellow silk banners hung overhead. I could hear the flapping of the wings of birds in the rafters.

Next to me, a man kneeled, and in one fluid motion he bent over, his forehead to the floor. The wide cedar planks had been scrubbed so many times they were smooth and soft, and a sudden shaft of sunlight turned them to silver. Smoke from the incense made the light palpable. Slowly, a white feather drifted down.

In the silence, broken only by the rustle of a monk's robe, I stopped and listened. I watched the rhythm of my breath steaming from my nostrils. Up so high in the thin, cold air of the Himalayan plateau, even the holy water had frozen in the stone basin. Time expanded as I looked around. It was the moment that justified thousands of miles of travel, when all my senses came alive as I drank in the scene.

We can take the traveler's eye into our everyday environment. Imagine if you could transfer the intensity you feel in an exotic situation to the experience of first entering a room. Your heightened senses key into the sounds and sights of a new place, and you become aware of how light hits the floor and how shadows collect in the corners.

You come to understand the soul of a space.

It's all about learning to see.

Published by Artisan
A Division of Workman Publishing, Inc.
708 Broadway
New York, New York 10003-9555
www.artisanbooks.com

Library of Congress Cataloging-in-Publication Data
Wolf, Vicente.
Learning to see : bringing the world around you into your home / text and photographs, Vicente Wolf.
p. cm.
ISBN 1-57965-217-4
1. Interior decoration. I. Title.
NK2115.W828 2002
747—dc21   2002074605

Printed in Singapore
10 9 8 7 6 5 4 3

Project Editor, Joseph Montebello
Book Design, Lisa Yee

Le

arning to See

foreword BY LOUIS OLIVER GROPP 10
point of view 15 thinking like a designer 25
plan 39 space 57 form 75 color 113 light 137
texture 161 home 177 acknowledgments 195
resources 196

THOSE OF US WHO HAVE APPRECIATED Vicente Wolf's cool, luminous rooms over the twenty-five years of his career can only be grateful that this interior designer/photographer/world traveler has taken the time to share the insight behind the strong, sensuous interiors for which he is known. Born in Cuba, Vicente moved to New York City, where he immersed himself in the city's rich troves of art and design, fashion and style, mining it for skills he would later use in the world of interior design.

Joining forces with design partner Bob Patino—they would work together for fifteen years—their work soon began appearing in the pages of *House & Garden* and *House Beautiful*. Those early rooms document the consistency of Vicente's vision, a vision that has been enriched by his frequent travels and his growing involvement with photography. Whether capturing the lightness and freshness of rooms in the palaces of Sweden or the minimalism and modernity of a Shaker village, Wolf's special gift is his acute visual sensibility.

In this remarkably personal volume, Vicente shares his belief that we can find our own style by becoming conscious of the things that bring us pleasure. In

foreword

the process he also shares his understanding of the basic skills required in creating beautiful rooms: working with space, color, and materials; devising a furniture plan that is flexible; maintaining design consistency without boredom.

Vicente Wolf is a designer who doesn't ever want to be boxed in, who prefers rooms where you can add a couple of 1950s lean chairs from Copenhagen or a pompous Italian sofa that you found by chance and happen to love, without bringing down the whole. A successful space for Vicente is always in motion, "an open system that can be visited by the occasional shooting star."

Change keeps a room alive, according to Vicente. The practical advice included in the pages of this book will teach you how he does it. But the pleasure will come from joining him on his personal journey of discovery, the secrets he shares, his unexpected ways of thinking about things and life. This is a book about one man's special way of seeing and his response to what he sees.

LOUIS OLIVER GROPP

point of view

Buildings taught me something about the nature of Cuba—
and my own nature—when I was growing up. They awakened
my senses to the pageant of penetrating light, tropical color,
and the patina of time. Certain images are still filed away in
my mind—how sunlight traveled through panes of colored
glass in old colonial homes, or the way luminous beams inched
across the stones of the cathedral during mass, revealing all
the veins and pores of its worn surfaces.

One of the houses in the countryside where I grew up was built in 1910. I vividly remember the
impression of bright green light just outside the door to the garden and shadows playing on the coral
stone walls. The textures picked out by the sun taught me to admire the luster that time gives to wood
and stone. Even the configuration of the table in the dining room—a long mahogany table jammed
with chairs and surrounded by thick walls—added to the pleasures of our family gatherings. The room
made me feel the energy of the company.

Nobody knew at the time, least of all me, that I was dyslexic. As a young boy, I already was compensating
for my difficulty with books in school by reading the environment around me. I learned to learn by
seeing. If you have no legs, you build up your arms to pull yourself along. Somehow, dyslexia drove me to
cultivate my senses, especially vision. As a child, I embarked on what has become a lifelong alternative
education. My gift of being able to see things so clearly comes from depending on my mind's eye.
By the age of thirteen, I was haunting the Museum of Modern Art in Havana, finding solace in the colors
and composition of the paintings and admiring their ornate frames. My difficulties with the printed word
pushed me into the visual world of imagination and make-believe. I pored over copies of the *National
Geographic*; the images took me to places I vowed to see someday.

Growing up in old Havana, I was surrounded
by history. On my way to school, I passed part of
the colonial fortifications.

My father and mother imported building materials. Many of their friends were architects, so construction sites became as familiar to me as playgrounds were to most other children. I was aware of floor plans and used to draw them out for myself, imagining spaces in my mind. In the loneliness caused by my learning disability, I dwelled in my own little world, arranging things, making order. At home, I'd spend hours playing in my room with imaginary friends and moving the furniture around. I was pushing chairs and tables as though reshuffling toys, but they were the props of my fantasies. Interior design was a career I didn't even know existed. Arranging furniture was like a very calming meditation, and it came to me naturally. Shortly before we left Cuba, my parents bought a new house. On the morning we moved in, the furniture arrived just as they were leaving for work. By the time they came home, I had arranged the whole house.

When you're young, you have so little to say about where life takes you. I was fifteen when my parents decided to leave Cuba, and when we landed in Miami Beach in 1961, I went into culture shock. We arrived with what we could carry. Mother took the photograph albums and a few boxes of objects that were precious to her. Then I watched her sell those few things because we had to get money to eat. They were the things I had loved and grown up with. This was our heritage, our collective memory, in a box.

I was excited to be in a country I had always had so much fun visiting. Only now it was a different reality. I had little education and no preparation to earn a living. When I got to New York I felt a sense of arriving at last where I wanted to be, but still had no idea of how to find my place there. I didn't know anybody. I walked through museums, making friends with the paintings at the Metropolitan Museum of Art. I haunted the period rooms, seeing styles of furniture that were new to me. It was like traveling around the world within the walls of one museum. I could get lost in ancient or medieval art. The city itself was another kind of animated museum. I walked on avenues surrounded by a sense of luxury and style. New York became my new *National Geographic*.

It was an awakening and a frustration at the same time. I didn't need to retreat into the dream world inside my head anymore. My dream world was all around me. I went from job to job, jumping among advertising, banking, modeling,

White walls and white furniture have been part of my life since I was a child. In my grandmother's house, I was mesmerized by the way light came through those squares of colored glass and played over the walls. The scent of roses and gardenias outside my window woke me up every morning. At our country house my parents kept monkeys, goats, chickens, horses, and a hundred-year-old turtle.

selling—and acting, which was utterly hopeless because I couldn't memorize lines. I worked at Bergdorf Goodman when Halston was designing hats. I was trying everything, desperate to find a career, but there aren't so many opportunities for someone without an education. It was not as if I had little skill; I had no skill at all. I was truly lost.

I was also socially inept, but lucky enough to meet my future design partner, Bob Patino, who was then working as a showroom salesperson for a fabric house. By observing the path he had taken, for the first time I saw a direction and a sense of purpose. I got a job working with interior designers in a fabric showroom. By a stroke of luck, I had circled back to an old pastime from my childhood— planning interiors and doing drawings. I had been slow to find this point again, but once I did, my life accelerated. One day I was sweeping floors in a showroom. A year later my first decorating job appeared in *House Beautiful*.

As I started designing, I returned to what I did best—observing, letting my eye wander on the streets, in gardens, in museums. I transcribed the memories and put them to work in real environments. I was influenced by David Hicks, Billy Baldwin, and, of course, Bob, with whom I worked for fifteen years. What he gave me was an incredible opportunity. He opened the door—into myself, really—and put me in touch with my own creativity. I learned to appreciate what I saw, and to understand what I liked and what I didn't like.

Not being able to read easily, the knowledge and opinions of "authorities" was often beyond my reach. I usually had to rely solely on my own judgment, and my independence became a pattern. I once enrolled in design school, but when the teacher said curtains should be an inch off the floor, I said no. Instinctively, I believe curtains should break on the floor and overlap an inch. I walked out and never went back.

As a designer, I've learned to be guided by the pleasure principle. I have trained myself to seize that moment when I notice something beautiful, to understand just why it appeals and how the principles can be applied to design. I design through an associative visual logic; the patina on an old stucco wall in Morocco might translate to rough and tactile fabrics in a Manhattan living room.

I believe you can find your own style simply by becoming conscious of the things that bring you pleasure. The path to wisdom, it has been said, is self-knowledge. You can cultivate your own likes and experiences—the colors in a favorite painting, the textures of shells discovered on a beach—and translate these pleasures into the design of your own home. I am encouraging not imitation, but independence. I will show you how you can empower yourself and develop the confidence of your own eye.

This book is not a how-to manual. You won't come away able to lay a parquet floor or sew your own curtains. But I hope you will find it rich in ideas for your home. My thoughts are meant to be an example of finding your inner self—getting in touch not so much with my creativity, but with your own.

As far as I have traveled from my roots, they're still so much a part of me. Whenever I'm on the beach looking up at the blue sky, I'm right back to that free and easy life of a child. Everything has a freshness and lightness that I try to convey in my interiors.

thinking

like a designer

There are two people in me fighting to get out. One person is the Cuban exile, and the other is the professional who organizes space. Each brings something different to the design equation. The professional comes equipped with experience, a filing cabinet of ideas, a Rolodex of sources, and a methodical way of working through a job.

The Cuban spontaneously jumps at the chance to play into a client's fantasies and look at things in fresh ways; he wants to throw out the tried-and-true solution favored by the professional. My two halves often argue with each other but finally come to terms. This creates an interesting tension that results in a design full of surprises, and still balanced and sharp.

Not having any formal training puts me—and most other people looking at an empty room—at what could be considered an advantage. Since I don't feel bound by rules and conventions, I am committed to having an open mind, to operating outside the box. This I do mostly by keeping my eyes open. Whether it is a storefront window display or the set of a new play, I am constantly browsing the visual environment, making connections, storing ideas. My eyes work overtime on my trips, and what I absorb abroad usually comes out in a new form in my work.

On my first trip to Sweden, I walked through the palaces and wondered what made them special. Was it the extraordinary craftsmanship? The precious materials? The enormously grand spaces? I realized that the rooms didn't actually get much light and that the materials used were often very basic—they weren't as refined as those in eighteenth-century France. No, the life in those rooms came from a particularly Scandinavian coloration. The colors kept repeating—blue-greens, soft grays, whites, yellows. White seemed to take on different tones, depending on whether it was juxtaposed with a blue or a yellow. Touches of gold reflected light, and because the paint had a little age, the older colors seeped through the newer ones.

I gave traditional elegance a modern slant when I painted this country French daybed white and draped it in blue and white faille. White grosgrain ribbon trim on the cushions echoes the shape of the empty white frames on the wall. It's a provocative touch—my little homage to surrealism.

I think you should feel welcomed as soon as you walk into a house, with a place to hang your hat, sit down, and take off your sneakers. Shaker-esque furnishings strike a simple, straightforward note in the foyer of this Long Island beach house. The vertical lines of the early American ladder-back chair juxtaposed with the strong horizontal lines of the bench make a strong statement.

Back in New York, I wondered how to capture this lightness and freshness in my own rooms, especially when the sunlight just isn't there, and how to achieve the illusion of one color reading through another. I found myself borrowing a trick the Scandinavians employ to good advantage—using mirrors and chandeliers to catch the available light. I minimized window treatments to allow as much light as possible into the space. Layering things seemed one way to create a kind of spatial pentimento. That could mean simply putting something—a sculpture, a stack of baskets—beneath a table, half hiding it, or planning the geometry of a room so that a pale green chair emerges from behind a pale blue sofa as you walk around.

The first time I stepped into a Shaker village, I was completely blown away by how minimal and modern it was. How did these people, restrained by their religion from all usual forms of embellishment, create one of the most compelling periods in American design? How did they produce such a strong point of view with so few objects? These were people without training as artists or architects, but they knew what they wanted to say and how to say it in woods that were sanded, smoothed, and polished to reveal both the nature of the wood and the touch of their hand. If they needed a place to hang coats, they didn't construct an elaborate armoire; they just put up a rack with pegs. Each piece of Shaker furniture is perfectly plain and utterly functional, and therein lies power and beauty.

I asked myself if there was a way to bring this sense of simplicity and unpretentious honesty to my own work and still provide all the things necessary for today's lifestyle. I look at Shaker cabinetry, its godlike proportions and that balance, and come away with certain lessons—the shading and texture of the wood, perhaps, and the outlines—that I can reinterpret. I'm always trying to take a classic and make it look modern.

What I try to do is build a room around an emotion, a mood, or an idea. In a breakfast room, do I want to feel a sense of the sun on my face when I pour the coffee, even though the room faces north? In a bedroom, do I want to feel center stage? Exposed? Veiled? Enveloped?

PAGE 30: I built a freestanding curved mahogany wall to create a foyer and conceal the view so you don't see everything as soon as you enter this Manhattan apartment. There's a sense of discovery—you're propelled forward because you want to find out what's behind the wall. The steel-and-granite table is a contrast to the eighteenth-century Italian chair, and the ottoman covered in bright yellow Thai silk adds a splash of color.

PAGE 31: I wanted this library to feel like a warm cocoon, so everything is covered in chocolate brown. The color varies with each texture—the strié paint on the walls, the smooth leather sofa, the suede ottoman, the silk pillows, the velvet club chair. A mirror over the sofa reflects a collection of handcrafted burled wood bowls in the bookcase opposite.

How, for example, could I capture the sensual side of the Caribbean I love without being literal? You have to evoke it by alluding to its rhythms. You can't separate the rhythm from the dance, but you can make colors pulse through the space like a beat. Maybe the colors look like strong pastels that have faded in the sun. And humor, so much a part of the Caribbean personality, comes across in my work when the most unexpected things are used together: Breaking up propriety with something devilish and piquant. Being bad.

Using antiques—lively, individual pieces—in a room can make that room seem timeless. The right chair or table says charm, eccentricity, character in a way that most modern pieces can't. But antiques need to have a sense of humor, too. That's why I generally prefer Italian over French pieces. French furniture is formal, rigid, and academic compared to the more exuberant Italian. I often see personality in a chair, and if it is simpatico with mine, it's like finding a friend. I cherish the idea that the piece has traveled through time and still maintained its individuality.

You might want to suggest a sense of history in your decor, but how to do that in a new house? In one project at the beach, I wanted to convey the feeling that the rooms had been there for some time, but that it was still a contemporary environment. I brought in a French limestone mantel and coffered the ceiling, but in a geometric way so that you felt a dialogue between the contemporary lines and the antique style. I picked dark wicker furniture with a vintage flavor, and arranged it against a clear, spare, white background. I put old-fashioned lampshades on new sconces I designed. I never overwhelm a room with furniture from any one period, but I use enough older pieces to create a tension between the historical and the modern. A telephone sitting on a nineteenth-century side table won't look like an anachronism if you freely mix styles and periods throughout the room.

This boudoir is a blend of classical lines and whimsical touches. A traditional makeup table gets a coquettish update with inverted pleats, laced up and lined with white faille. The crisscross of white grosgrain ribbon on the seven-panel screen is graphic and functional—photographs and other personal memorabilia can be tucked under it, creating an ever-changing display.

LEFT: A small bathroom becomes chic with one simple gesture—black bands of grosgrain ribbon on the shower curtain, towels, and robe. It was all inspired by a Chanel No. 5 perfume package.

RIGHT: You can really appreciate the gilded curves of this bench when you see it against the more sober silhouette of the ebonized table.

OPPOSITE: I don't see the point of stiff, separate dining rooms. This dining area is more like a conversational corner, with a sofalike banquette and two slipcovered armchairs.

PAGE 36: Here's a characteristic mix of furniture—a Mies van der Rohe chaise longue, a neoclassical Italian armchair, and an African stool. The centuries and styles mingle in what ends up being a quintessentially modern space. Against the wall is one of my signature leaning mirrors.

PAGE 37: A flirtatiously skirted armchair and a shapely French table add a casual charm to this library.

plan

A happy few can walk into a room for the first time and intuitively envision a floor plan. They know exactly where the furniture should be placed. But I actually don't like to stand in the room and try to design it. There is just too much to process all at once if you are looking at the paneling, the radiator, and an ugly carpet. I find it best to work from a plan of the space on paper.

Instead of being bombarded by distractions, you can clear your mind and really see the space when you're staring at a clean piece of paper.

A little research goes a long way. Come to the drawing board with a library of images already in your mind's eye. You know what furniture you currently own and want to keep. But browse through the shelter magazines, skim through catalogs, and snoop around flea markets and furniture showrooms to get a sense of what is out there. You need not commit to anything, but the exercise will give you some reference points. You may find a piece you want to feature, or even build the room around.

At the same time, interview yourself; examine your lifestyle. How do you see the room being used? If it's for entertaining, do you usually have small or large groups? Will the guests casually mill around and mingle or sit down in committed seating arrangements? Don't make our parents' mistake and construct one of those picture-perfect living rooms with matching furniture that went stale because no one ever stepped past the unwritten KEEP OUT sign at the door. The message was very clear: This room is just to look at.

Every room does not have to center on a fireplace. Here you want to sit by the light and look out at the trees, which makes this corner the perfect place for an L-shaped sofa.

DRAWING A PLAN

- Using a tape measure, determine the dimensions of the room. Draw the room to half-inch scale (a half inch equals one foot). Make sure your floor plan of the room includes doors, windows, the fireplace, and other fixed features.

- Measure your furniture and draw it at half-inch scale on another sheet of paper. Then cut out the pieces.

- Using your cutouts, experiment with different layouts. Push and pull the pieces, almost kneading the plan. You will find yourself bumping into dimensional realities: That sofa will fit along some walls but not others. The space will not allow for a chaise longue if you insist on a pair of love seats in addition to the sofa.

- The more you shuffle the cutouts on the drawing and in your imagination, the more you realize that rooms have their own physics. While steering the sofa clear of the traffic, keep it as near the daylight as possible. There is always a subtle relationship between the furniture you choose and the plan into which it fits. Generally, if I had to argue for the chicken or the egg, I would side with the egg. The floor plan is going to dictate the form and type of furniture.

PAGE 43: It makes sense to place a reading chair near a window. Always make sure there's a good lamp close by, as well as a table where you can set down a book or a drink.

Instead of one grouping in front of the fireplace, I split this room up into two seating areas to utilize the full expanse of space. The repetition of the same shapes in the sofas and club chairs and the same fabrics—soft wool, leather, linen, and velvet—helps unify the furniture plan.

Now that you have drawn your plans, you understand the shell. You know its strong and weak points—features such as the fireplace, the southern exposure, the long view, the ten-foot ceiling, and challenges such as too many doors or awkwardly proportioned windows. The meanest problem is downright basic—a room that is simply too small. Some features will actually conflict, and the furniture plan will have to resolve the spatial argument. For example, the furniture should make way for traffic patterns so people won't be cutting

LEFT: Instead of one coffee table, I chose two for flexibility. I bought the 1940s gilded bronze table with the black marble top in Paris, then made a more modern version to scale. A pair of tables doesn't always have to match; the tables just have to speak to each other.

RIGHT: I'm always mixing straight lines and curves. The rounded shapes of the sofa and chair look even more lush next to a rectangular table.

OPPOSITE: The voluptuously curved sofa is so inviting it pulls you into this room. The curve is a nice counterpoint to the neoclassical lines of the fireplace.

through conversational groupings. A floor plan with good manners can correct rude interruptions.

Usually, you can get a workable solution on the first pass, but hold that thought. There are probably better, more interesting plans. The challenge is to push yourself to find mature, evolved arrangements that may not be apparent on the first round. You want not just an adequate solution but the best

Built-in bookshelves balance
the door on the other side of the
fireplace by mimicking its
proportions. A tight corner
becomes more useful with the
addition of an eighteenth-century
Chinese table that can catch the
overflow and organize it into
another display. A 1950s model
of an atom sits on the other
side of the fireplace.

solution. Work the pieces of paper until you get configurations that are unexpected. Surprise yourself.

As you pencil in the outlines, always keep thinking about what you feel, or want to feel, in the space. Rooms must start with an emotion; without a personal investment, they turn cold.

The idea of matched furniture settings somehow haunts our imagination—the large imposing sofa coordinated with a pair of reading chairs persists across America. But why not try something different? I like to compose in vignettes, creating two or more smaller groupings in a room, with pieces from different periods and cultures. Vignettes are more flexible in a plan than a single monolithic grouping.

There is no formula for these smaller groupings other than the principle of mixing disparate things and supporting some kind of real activity. You are a reader. You might construct a vignette in a corner around a deep, battered leather club chair, under a standing lamp with a warm parchment shade—a place to spend hours. A side table for the mug of coffee that keeps you company also holds a stack of books and a beautiful seashell. The tabletop may itself be the site of another, smaller vignette—perhaps a favorite collection becomes a whole tablescape.

BENDING THE RULES I am not the sort of designer who abides by the classic rules. It is more fun to reinvent rooms than to just apply received wisdom. The dining room is a case in point. By the time you add up the dimensions of the table, chairs, walk-around space, and a sideboard, there is only one configuration possible. Besides, a table with eight chairs is almost incurably static; it leaves no room for imagination. Most of the time it is bare. When it is set, it is usually equally boring with matching plates and silver, and that predictable chandelier centered over it. The traditional configuration does not allow for much flexibility.

I try to use unmatched chairs to break the sameness, or a banquette on one side and chairs on the other to make the room less predictable. I love complexity, and think of the dining table as a stage waiting for props. I like

Whether a room is formal or informal, it is much more interesting to have a mixed group of chairs around the dining table than a matched set. With a little two-seat sofa and two place settings at either end, you can double the conversational possibilities.

to see lots of colors on the table, a mix of china, silver, and glass styles. Candles add a lot of diversity, not to mention drama.

A rectangular living room does not automatically have to have a rectangular seating plan. I may arrange a square grouping of furniture on a rug. In general, though, I like to define distinct areas in a room with rugs, which is a more subtle way of staking out territory than reconfiguring walls or changing colors. A rug elasticizes space; it can make a room feel bigger or smaller.

I avoid static configurations that stop the eye. My vignettes may have a centerpiece but not because it's in the center: The piece is simply the most prominent within a hierarchy of asymmetrically arranged parts. I'll juxtapose a tufted ottoman with a smoothly upholstered sofa, or throw in a boudoir chair whose diminutive scale and feminine curves enhance the mix. Generally I prefer groupings composed of odd rather than even numbers. Odd numbers tend to keep the space in a room moving—even at a dinner party because three are more dynamic than two. I find self-contained settings stay empty more than asymmetrical vignettes, which open up the room.

It is all right to have one formal setting, such as a sofa and two chairs and a cocktail table, but I always do something somewhere to throw in a bit of a curve, either within the setting itself or in another part of the room.

Somehow we are brainwashed by our boxy buildings into thinking that the right angle is divine. But I find the devil in the diagonal, and it is always interesting. Angling a chaise or reading chair toward a corner changes the direction of a room. If you are continually seeing the room from a diagonal point of view, it fools the eye into thinking the room is bigger. Diagonals add dynamism to the balance of elements in a space.

I like the idea of a round table in a square room. A round table makes conversation easier. With nobody presiding over the head of the table, everybody's equal. The shirred silk lampshade is deliberately overscaled, for impact, and creates an intimate cone of light at night.

PAGE 54: A sea-grass rug defines a large entrance foyer. Central to the shape is a table I designed with big bold S curves, inspired by a seventeenth-century William and Mary scroll-leg table.

PAGE 55: A secondary set of stairs to the second floor of this Los Angeles house was sealed off to create a usable niche. The sofa was built to fit the space, then both the sofa and walls were upholstered in the same fabric to create a little cocoon. The mirror was added to keep the niche from feeling claustrophobic.

space

Before I even flirt with furniture, I try to understand the character of the empty space. I interrogate the house or apartment in the same way I question clients. How does light enter the space? Are the ceilings high or low? What are the architectural features? Where are the views? Do the walls need to be reconfigured? The idea is to turn deficits into assets, and emphasize the existing pluses.

The designers I admire most treat interior space as a kind of three-dimensional frame for furniture that they deploy like sculpture. In order to make that work, I first have to establish the clarity of a room's volume. I'm not sentimental about decoration, so I just strip out moldings if they're weak. Often all they do is add extra lines you really don't want to see. Even the modest contractor molding around doors and floors in bland 1950s houses can distract the eye. Similarly, I remove valances that hang above windows at awkward heights. I'm ruthless about stripping away what seem like well-intended details when they interfere with the unity of the room. I want to get down to a clean, well-proportioned shell.

Some rooms have real architectural problems. A jittery floor plan, with walls moving in and out and forming awkward alcoves and niches, weakens the volume and takes away that sense of boundary against which a piece of furniture needs to play. Strong pieces deserve a good backdrop. If a room isn't regular, square it by filling in alcoves, for example, with closets or bookcases. A running shelf gives a wall a horizontal line that can help belt the space, making it feel tighter and more contained. Making the space square or rectangular gives a sense of containment; with defined boundaries, a room somehow looks bigger.

The strong horizontals of the wall-to-wall bookshelves and picture rail fool the eye into thinking this space is wider than it is. A dark metal screen, hung with a photograph, masks an awkward view of the back of the television.

You can further push the sense of a room being one big space by wrapping its walls, ceilings, and floors in a single color. Even if the floor plan is not so simple, you can give the appearance of unity—and expand the room—with a monochromatic palette that masks many sins. Blend the windows into the walls with shades the color of the walls. The strategy helps establish a continuity. Complete the wrapping of a room by bleaching or staining the floor, or laying a wall-to-wall carpet to match. The floors simply disappear into the walls and ceiling; you don't really know where one ends and the other begins.

By neutralizing the perimeter and keeping everything off the pale walls, the space seems to expand forever, creating a feeling of lightness, spareness, and calm, even in rooms with a full quota of furniture. Wraparound color, especially if it's white, sets off the furniture—and people—and liberates the pieces so that they float away from the wall, toward the center. A clean light shell looks modern.

Correcting a run-of-the-mill room with no "there" there can sometimes be done with design moves halfway between architecture and furniture. When you're sitting in a living room with a view of the dining table, you're looking at an absence, a room waiting to happen. The emptiness drains off the energy because the whole space feels less than full. If an open plan is too undefined, subdivide the space with a freestanding wall, perhaps with a built-in cabinet on one side, to give more definition, intimacy, and a little mystery to each side.

Give better definition to a room by bracketing either end with the same piece of furniture—a screen, mirror, or a pair of anything big enough to read across the space.

When you have simplified the shell, what's left really matters. You can make a lot of moves that influence the architecture without ever committing the house to major surgery. And when a room is disciplined, pure, and clear, it invites the grand gesture and the broad stroke.

SIMPLE SOLUTIONS TO TIGHT SPACES A lot of 1950s-style houses are coming up for renovation, and their low horizon line inside makes them constraining. In my house in Montauk, I stripped the rooms completely, taking out the baseboards and contractor molding. I took out the header over the door into

In my own house at the beach, everything is slipcovered in simple white cotton duck, so the furniture seems to evaporate and the space to expand.

PAGE 62: In my dining room, I replaced a small window with a wall of glass so you have the sensation of being right on top of the ocean while you are eating. A second table is draped to the floor and laden with books, but when necessary the two can be joined to accommodate a large group.

PAGE 63: A four-foot by eight-foot mirror behind a sofa brings the ocean into my beach house and doubles the sense of space. For a moment, it seems as if there is another window there. Only a photograph propped against the mirror breaks the illusion.

The canopy bed, which doubles as a sofa during the day, rises high enough to suit the lofty proportions of this space. The stark wrought-iron frame is like a line drawing in space, so strong that the room needs little other decoration. The rest of the furniture is equally interesting. A gilded bronze table blossoms in the center, surrounded by two 1950s Italian chairs, one slipcovered in an iridescent bronze fabric. A dining chair slipcovered in white gauze can go back to the table when guests arrive. African blowguns, for shooting darts, march across the mantel.

the living room to give the low ceilings some verticality, and to create continuity between rooms. Then I broke out the satin paint. I lacquered all the hallways, so that the walls reflected off each other, and then buffed the ceilings to a satin sheen. With the reflections, you don't know where the ceiling stops and the walls begin. This gives the illusion of height. I don't recommend a high gloss on the floors because it's not going to last and it shows all the dust. I'd rather see shiny ceilings, which take your eyes up, than shiny floors, which take your eyes down. When I want to raise the ceiling visually, I use window treatments that go all the way up in the space above the window, to give a room that extra lift and to make the wall continuous, floor to ceiling. That helps the wrap.

One of my most interesting projects was a Greenwich Village studio apartment that measured only seventeen by twenty-two feet, but had a thirteen-foot-high ceiling. When I walked into the room, it felt like a perfect cube. My strategy was to do just enough to bring out its character while retaining the original charm and scope of the space.

The apartment still had the original crown moldings and baseboards, which in New York after a century of paint jobs can be a mixed blessing. I cleaned them up and upgraded the flawed sections without elaborating. There was no need to beef up the moldings. I wasn't "restoring" the apartment to make it look older or more genteel; age wasn't the most exciting aspect of this space. I was trying to clarify its physical stature. Too much molding would have trivialized the space with pretension.

All it needed was a few touches. I lined the open-weave linen curtains with a black fabric. This formed a graphic stripe at the edge, which guided the eye up like a gestural line drawing in space. A Parentisi floor-to-ceiling lamp accentuated the height with another, finer line. The idea was to activate the full volume of the space, even in its upper reaches, expanding the apparent size of the room.

Then, as though it were a big bowl of space, I floated objects inside. Too many pieces would have made it impossible to appreciate the clarity and integrity of the space, but luckily my client had a connoisseur's eye. He already owned an

LEFT: A pair of screens brackets a console table that doubles as a dining table in this one-room apartment. To break the monotony of the four chairs, I slipcovered one, letting its black shoulders peek through.

RIGHT: I created a foyer in this apartment where there wasn't one, by using bed hangings as a backdrop for this nineteenth-century French inlaid rosewood table. A Japanese lacquer tray catches keys. The metal lamp formerly resided in a dentist's office.

OPPOSITE: Floor-to-ceiling curtains in cream-colored linen play up the height of the space—especially when the leading edge is trimmed with a vertical band of black.

intriguing mix of objects that hopscotched continents and decades—French art deco, eighteenth-century English, contemporary African. I composed them into self-contained vignettes so as not to clutter the space. The bed, heaped with pillows, became a luxurious sofa during the day. Its tall black wrought-iron frame—hung with more diaphanous linen in the minimalist's version of a canopied four-poster—reiterated the dimensions of the space, creating a virtual cube within the cube.

Few of us live in rooms that aspire to such height, but even tight spaces can be significantly improved. In a way, it is more gratifying to reinvent a contractor-built 1960s beach house or a cramped apartment in a vanilla building than a house already equipped with gorgeous bones and aristocratic bearing—not that I'm ready to give those up. When you're fortunate enough to be working on a great space, sometimes it's more interesting to hold yourself back. Like a beautiful woman who knows not to overdress, you can play down the space and let the natural features come through. You're complementing the space, not starting over.

MIRRORS From the splendors of the Hall of Mirrors at Versailles to the infinite regressions of Adolf Loos's tiny American Bar in Vienna, mirrors have had a long and distinguished tradition of dazzling the eye and expanding space. At their best they're magical.

But some people use mirrors like aspirin, to cure any room's headache. Too small? Too claustrophobic? Double it with reflections. Too predictable? Toss in an illusion. Frequently, mirrors become a design cliché.

You might be tempted to expand a small room, such as a bath, by mounting a big mirror. For maximum effect the mirror should be mounted wall to wall and floor to ceiling so that there's no awkward leftover space. Above a fireplace, you should mount a mirror over the whole chimney from edge to edge, and not just over the mantel.

But be cautious when you're using a big expanse of mirror. This works well only when what is reflected is worth reflecting: You don't want to see twice what isn't interesting once.

With the graceful sweep of the banister, the stair hall of this Connecticut country house was very beautiful and deserved something a little out-of-the-ordinary. Most people would have put one big thing—a painting or a mirror—on that large wall, but I decided to surprise the eye with three mirrors. Framed in black like the banister, they reflect slices of the space and create a perpetual sense of movement. A lampshade suspended from the ceiling over an architectural model of a staircase makes a witty statement.

With walls, cornice, and ceiling all painted white, and a gauzy scrim on the windows, the boundaries of this room blur and all attention focuses on the furnishings. When it came to the coffee table, I took a multilevel approach by placing a standard table over an ottoman, which allows you to put your feet up and still keep your coffee within arm's reach. The two rectangles create intersecting planes, and I added another rectangle with the mirror. The bold black lines of the mirror are echoed in grosgrain ribbon on the floor-length skirt of the side table and on the black band of the sisal rug.

Mirrors can create mystery or they can douse it. For example, they become too literal when you use them head-on. Use them glancingly, so that you're not walking squarely into an image of yourself. I like to see a reflection obliquely, so I don't usually put a mirror just opposite a door, but to its side. Never use a wall-to-wall mirror when a space is already large. It robs the room of intimacy and destroys any sense of containment, which is so important in creating that feeling of place.

A framed mirror the same height as a door can trick the mind into thinking there's another room beyond. It becomes a window into an imaginary view. You're not quite so interested in the reflection as you are in the illusion of breaking through a wall.

A mirror can be an object in itself. I might mirror a table, or stack three small antique mirrors next to a bed as a visual anecdote. But the right mirror in the right size can also amount to an architectural feature. If you rest a large full-length mirror in a husky frame on the floor, leaning against the wall, you can create the equivalent of a fireplace. Something about that gesture commands the space and reorients the room. The upturned image angles the room off into uncertainty, which is much more interesting than any straightforward reflection. The mirror becomes a spatial joker putting the room into play and giving it a different, very unexpected point of view.

The frame of the mirror can help you make a statement as well. The profile can be simple or elaborate, new or antique. Watch the proportions and the surfaces. A gilded frame catches light and enhances the mirror's sparkle. A dark wood frame is more modern and looks graphic against a light-colored wall. If the frame is substantial, the mirror works like a piece of furniture, and since you're not so interested in the reflection, you can put other furniture in front. The mirror is just one of the design layers, and the reflections multiply the effect.

This is not the focal wall in this room—that distinction usually belongs to the wall with the fireplace—but it becomes much more interesting when the door is flanked with two huge mirrors, each five feet square. They are an unexpected touch, and they throw the scale of the room off, in a provocative way—they are actually larger than the Anglo-Indian cabinets underneath. What could have been a mere passageway now has presence.

form

Shape matters, especially in white, uncluttered rooms. I like to take a piece of furniture and isolate it to reveal its form. But you have to make sure it merits the attention. In a stark, simple room, the burden of proof falls on the furniture. You want the pieces to combust with energy in a contained explosion of style.

It's counterintuitive, I admit, but somehow the simple shells I create invite complex furniture groupings. The calm sets the stage for a drama in which each piece has a dynamic role. I never lock a room into one particular period because consistency is boring. The only way to really appreciate a particular style is to juxtapose it with something from another period. For instance, a sturdy Arts and Crafts reading chair in leather and quarter-sawn oak and a sleek moderne armchair in velour and chrome are worlds and philosophies apart, but putting them next to each other creates sparks.

In my groupings, I embrace opposites—classic Edwardian-style curves and crisp modern profiles, straight and rounded backs, taut upholstery and loose cushions. Shapes must balance each other to form a coherent whole. If I choose a sofa that is loose-backed and brimming with pillows, next to it will be a tight-backed chair. A voluptuous tufted-leather ottoman might be paired with a primitive African bench hollowed from a tree trunk. Soft curves counter hard edges. A sofa with a rounded arm is balanced by chairs with square arms. The contrast creates drama. If you furnish everything in the same style, you have boxed yourself in. What if you pick up a couple of 1950s chairs in Copenhagen or drive across town and chance on an Italian sofa that is all pomp and circumstance, but your all-deco living room says no way. A mix gives you much more freedom to incorporate a new find without bringing down the whole ensemble. The point is not to create a rigidly uniform whole, or even a perfect, don't-change-a-thing whole, but a dynamic combination based on the idea of change.

The elegant vertical lines of that high-backed eighteenth-century chair, slipcovered in pale blue cotton, play against the more languid horizontal planes of the contemporary sofa. The solid blocks of color stand out against the patterned carpet and set up a balance so the exuberant rug doesn't overpower the space. The shiny lacquered ceiling reflects the light and makes the ceiling appear higher.

A successful space for me is always in motion. That is why it is important to blend different elements and periods. You do not want a closed constellation with only six planets in fixed places. You want a system that can be visited by the occasional shooting star. Change keeps a room alive.

Flexibility is almost as important as diversity. There are few things I love more than walking into a room and shoving furniture around into a new configuration—just for the fun of it, or because I am adding or subtracting a piece. You see the room, your day, even yourself differently.

Program flexibility into your rooms by devising sections that you know will change from time to time. It could be a tabletop of photos that new pictures encourage you to rearrange. Or a collection of Italian glass that is refreshed after your Sunday-morning foray to a flea market. Lean paintings and artwork on a picture rail attached to a wall instead of hanging them on hooks. You will find yourself moving them about much more, seeing new relationships among them. I like furniture that is actually on wheels. Whether it is a dining table or a coffee table, the ease of being able to roll the piece encourages movement. The environment becomes participatory. There is a wisdom in creating a space that invites your ongoing hands-on involvement.

At the Metropolitan Museum of Art, I always found Caravaggio a master of composition: Baroque painters were interested above all in space, in finding three dimensions in two. I admire the way he orchestrated high, medium, and low elements on his canvases. He overlapped colors and patterns and light and dark in front of each other, using dominant and recessive elements. He was a genius at spatial illusion, pushing and pulling elements from bottom to top, into and out of the depth of the canvas.

Gradations of height in a room are no different. If you are lucky enough to have a room ten to fifteen feet tall, you can introduce a mirror eight to ten feet high, along with floor-length curtains at the windows to play up the height. Try to create several heights that give the vertical dimension a complex balance. If you want two tables, for example, use two that have different heights. If you have a low ceiling, add something tall to pull up the room. Vary

PAGE 78: A hallway with a beautifully curved wall becomes a library with the addition of shelves and a massive mahogany table. The solid rectangular table offers a nice contrast to the curves.

PAGE 79: Opposites attract: The ornately carved nineteenth-century fireplace chair is the perfect foil for the sleek Eero Saarinen table. This anteroom to a master bedroom served no real purpose until I added a picture ledge that wraps the perimeter. Now it functions as a gallery. Setting the rug at an angle energizes the space.

OPPOSITE: This double-height space is taller than it is wide, which made it feel a little boxy. I added an eight-foot by twelve-foot mirror that virtually doubled the width of the room. Instead of centering the mirror on the wall, I took it right to the edge, which makes it feel more like a window.

the horizon line, because, oddly enough, keeping everything at one height makes a room look off balance. Up and down, back and forth: Keep pushing and pulling until you have explored the vertical potential of a space. Think of the different heights as discrete stepping-stones from the floor to the ceiling, so that you end up using the full height of the space.

ELEVATION DRAWINGS A floor plan will give you a sense of how a room should be arranged, but it is not the final word. While an architect generally organizes a room in a plan, an artist visualizes it head-on, depicting the whole as you would see it if you were stepping through the door.

Try to understand a space as both an architect and an artist, planning it and then visualizing it in what architects call elevations. These front-on renderings help you see how the furniture will look in the third dimension, in front of walls, windows, and moldings. They also help you see how the vignettes work within more open spaces.

This is the time to get specific with the pieces you want to use, because their shapes and colors mean more in an elevation study than in a floor plan. Always think in terms of contrasts: high, medium, and low; rough and smooth; leggy versus voluminous. I believe in furniture biodiversity: club chairs, slipper chairs, wing chairs. The character of each piece reads better in contrast to others. If a bed happens to have a curved prow, all the better. These exclamation points lift a room out of the ordinary.

Think of the compositions as mutable rather than rigid hierarchies. A room with contrasting elements can shift easily as your point of view changes. If, five or ten years from now, you are thinking more traditionally, you can emphasize the more traditional pieces. A room will have a longer life if your initial concept embraces change.

Elevations became part of my process after I studied Japanese landscape paintings, in which artists use a form of perspective called axonometric, which recedes in space in a way that lets you understand buildings simultaneously in plan and elevation. You are looking at both the basic organization and the facades at the same time. You also see how the layering of a space gives it depth.

I hung silk shades at the windows in this double-height living room to take the eye down and frame the view. The elaborate candlesticks contrast with the clean modern lines of the 1970s house. Their tarnished gold shimmers at night when the candles are lit and brings the luster of age to the space.

The elevations I find so helpful give a good approximation of what a room looks like straight on. Again, you usually prepare scale drawings, but this time they are not of the floor but of the walls. If you are handy with a camera and a photocopying machine, you can scale photographs of the furniture up or down and cut out the images to use in your compositions. It doesn't matter if, as a draftsman, you are equipped with two left hands. The gesture is what matters most—the relative height and width of the pieces, their silhouettes, their density in a room, the way they work with each other. Some designers do elaborate watercolor renderings to present to clients, but these are usually done after the basic decisions have already been worked out. You don't need to sell a plan to yourself with a formal drawing.

COMPOSING BY CONTRAST In a Park Avenue apartment I designed, you can get a good idea of the whole interior just by rapping on the door. At my favorite flea market in Paris, I found an eighteenth-century door knocker, mounted it on a flush, completely undecorated door, and lacquered the door black. Set in a frame with an elaborately profiled molding, the stark door is a stripped abstract plane that contrasts with the finely wrought brass hand. The entrance announces that the apartment beyond will be a dramatic mix of the traditional and the contemporary.

It was a privilege to design this grand penthouse, with its large living room and den, its high ceilings, abundant light, and impressive views of the city. This kind of apartment, crown moldings intact, used to be the province of buttoned-down stockbrokers, but there is a new generation of people with a younger aesthetic agenda now occupying these old white-glove buildings. My clients, a filmmaker and his wife, who own a collection of big, bold contemporary art, did not want a formal interior. The couple regularly entertain up to forty guests, and the wife gave me a very clear sense of the feeling they desired in the main space: It should seem like a glass of Champagne—sparkling and festive.

That is the kind of guiding idea a project should have—difficult to achieve, but challenging. It makes me strive to find the right metaphors in the material world. Inside in the entry foyer I continued the message of old and new. I

The mahogany table with the big S curves is deliberately overscale, to make a strong statement of its own as you walk into this Park Avenue foyer. The table is a traditional form treated in a contemporary way, which also describes my approach to the whole apartment. The paintings are by Francesco Clemente and Jean-Michel Basquiat.

You don't expect to see an
ebullient Venetian chandelier
over a strictly modern Eero
Saarinen table, but that's why
it works. It's the sheer delight of
the surprise, combined with the
fact that both objects represent
great design. A series of drawings
by Brice Marden hangs over the
fireplace, and fourteenth-century
Thai honey pots are arrayed on
the mantel. A nineteenth-century
Kirman rug adds a field of color
underfoot.

floated a heavy mahogany table off center, and its outsize, sculptural, S-shaped legs seem both baroque and modern at the same time. A tall, thin silver lamp from the 1920s has a strict delicacy that contrasts with the table's massive wood slabs. I kept the room's crown molding but blew out and enlarged the traditional doorways, creating high, wide passageways to echo the abstraction of that black front door. I replaced the dowdy parquet with a stained wide-plank floor that lets the eye glide between spaces. In other words, I cleaned up the eye-stopping fussiness, making it much more hospitable to the art—and to the furniture and guests, who now stand out in the clarity. You only pass through this room, but it is a microcosm of the rest of the apartment.

In the expansive living room, the lady of the house wanted light, watery green tones, and materials rich in texture. The furniture and art had to cohabit in the space without making it seem like a gallery. I began, as always, with the furniture plan. Rather than using the fireplace as a gathering point, I used it to divide the room into two parts for seating at either end. Billy Baldwin often dealt with large rooms by positioning a table in the middle, so I took a page from his book. I wanted a contemporary table to give the room focus, one that would look as if it had grown out of the floor. The Saarinen table, with the smooth, organic lines of a stalk, offered the perfect form to punctuate the center. I chose one with a black base and a green marble top.

One day, while I was working on the project, I chanced on an eighteenth-century Venetian glass chandelier hanging in a shop, and I knew it would be incredible in that space. It looked like a piece of jewelry, its tiers wired together with strands of crystal. Suspended directly over the Saarinen table, it makes an exuberant contrast to the table's smooth modernist simplicity.

My furniture plan called for chairs facing out from the table into the room. A lot of the design process is just keeping your eyes open as you focus on a job. On a trip to Houston, I found an opulent, gilded nineteenth-century Russian chair with curvaceous lines. I talked my way into buying it (it actually was not for sale) and brought it home. I reinterpreted the chair and had Sotheby's create three new ones. I upholstered the seats in textured linen without welts.

A Chinese coffee table looks right at home near a Victorian papier-mâché side table in this corner of the living room. The rich mix of color and texture continues in the upholstery and curtains. Instead of merely framing the windows, I took the silk taffeta all the way to the walls because I wanted the block of color.

PAGE 90: Mahogany paneling sets a deep, dark tone in the library. Simple metal stands hold African dowry bracelets, arrayed on a table that moves up and down as needed for dining or drinks. The painting is by Sean Scully.

PAGE 91: The dining room becomes slightly mysterious and very romantic with walls draped in silk taffeta. I designed the table to break up into four smaller tables that can seat eight people each. Instead of a uniform ring of dining chairs, I used a mix of styles. The 1940s needlepoint chairs by Jules Leleu were just the right fanciful touch. Mirrored "sconces" are on wheels so they can be rolled up to the table for an intimate dinner. The painting is by Ross Bleckner.

In the bedroom, I juxtaposed old and new, traditional and modern, yin and yang once again. The eighteenth-century French table covered with silk velvet is topped with a slab of glass for twenty-first-century practicality. A little Japanese altar table holds a collection of English silver. Three eighteenth-century Italian mirrors hang on the wall. The oak storage cube underneath introduces a purely modern element.

Circling the Saarinen table, the three new chairs add another contrasting layer of style to the table and chandelier.

The space had to work for both small and large gatherings, and the two intimate furniture groups clustered at opposite ends of the room leave the majority of space open for milling guests. At one end, I created a classic arrangement, with a sofa flanked by two large chairs. At the other end, I placed a more informal L-shaped, tufted sofa, which elbowed around a low Chinese table. The yin and yang of these two arrangements—one symmetrical, one not—gives the space its tension. The two groupings are united in that both sofas are upholstered in silver sage and the chairs in natural buckskin. A Japanese gilded altar table, a nineteenth-century art nouveau vase, wooden cookie molds from the Himalayas, a Chinese trunk, and an African mask add variety to the space.

The single most important piece that gives the room its Champagne is a huge Kirman rug, which also ties it all together. Instead of finding something that matched the plain velvet upholstery of the sofas, I chose a lighter rug with an evanescing woven wool surface. The colors change as you see it from different angles in different lights. You sense that you are walking on shallow green and blue pools of shimmering water. The eye rises from the carpet, which grounds the room, into the white lightness above. The Champagne bubbles reside in the chandelier.

For consistency in the design, but without boredom, I took the same color and material palette into the other rooms, shifting it slightly. Tones in the living room were at the surface. In the library, I used the aqueous colors but went down further in the water level to deeper hues. I upholstered the sofas in a greenish-gray and the ottoman and reading chair in a leather whose iridescence kept them from becoming too solid and massive. Since the room is used primarily at night, I paneled the walls in mahogany to create an enveloping quality. I designed the table to move up and down like a piston, depending on whether it is used for cocktails or dining.

In the bedroom, those silver-green tones from the living room go lighter. I wrapped the floor and walls in the same color (the walls are upholstered in a ribbed silk), and carried the color into the apron of the bed. The bed was the centerpiece of the room, and I framed it asymmetrically with three small eighteenth-century Italian mirrors that I found in Germany, and a gilded eighteenth-century table from Paris. A huge mirror leans against a wall behind a dresser, throwing the whole space into play.

BEDTIME No room comes charged with more complex associations than the bedroom, and you have to decide just where to set the dial on its emotional temperature. This is the place in a house where you are most vulnerable. You dress and undress here; the room itself almost takes over the role of your clothing, providing comfort, privacy, reassurance, and pleasure. It can be anything from a protective cocoon to a sanctum sanctorum of sensuality. Just for you, or the two of you together.

Color plays an important part in creating environmental moods everywhere in the house, and especially in the bedroom. I often use wall-to-wall carpet in fleshy tones to soften the room and wrap the space in color. To emphasize the sense of touch, I often upholster the walls in soft, tactile textures with an even coloration, often a beige tending to a blush. This is the room where you sit without much clothing. The right textures talk to your senses; they should be kind.

The design of a bedroom really begins with the bed. It's hard to work around this piece of furniture, usually the room's biggest. The best way is to celebrate it, to make the most of it. Siting it in an interesting way is half the battle. Choosing beautiful linens is the other half.

Configure the space so that when you step into the room, you encounter the bed straight on, from the foot, and see this pile up of softness: first the comforter, then the pillows, the headboard, and perhaps a standing screen or upholstered or paneled walls. The layered sequence cumulatively forms a picture of a personal, evocative room. Each element complements the next, inviting your eye more deeply into the space. When you see a bed from the side without this buildup, it loses all the lushness.

If you can't site the bed for a head-on approach, configure the plan so that you approach it from an interesting angle, as though positioning a face to the

In a room without any real architectural features, I needed a focal point. So I chose a graphic Chinese screen for a headboard and mirrored the back to get that extra gleam of light. The sculptural Isamu Noguchi table adds another twist to the grid of the screen. At the foot of the bed, a rough African bed made of wood serves as a magazine stand. African chieftain's staffs are displayed on the nightstand.

OPPOSITE: It is possible to have a canopy bed without a canopy. In this bedroom, a recessed panel in the ceiling hides the curtain rods and gives an old-fashioned concept a clean, straight line. The hangings are made of taupe wool faille banded with grosgrain ribbon and lined in white. The curved chenille sofa brings softness to a very linear room.

If you want to instantly make a bedroom more interesting, try moving the bed into the center of the room. In this house in Natchez, Mississippi, a free-floating bed becomes a sculptural object and gives this 1840s room a sense of contemporary spaciousness. I was thinking of a classical column when I designed the gilded night table.

camera in quarter profile. If there is enough space, try floating it so that it stands free of the walls. This way it acquires a fourth side and becomes the centerpiece of the room. A screen placed behind it can provide the privacy of the missing wall. I sometimes build the room around the bed, using other furniture to change the context so that it becomes a multipurpose room centered on a daybed. It is not solely a bedroom anymore. Don't always look at the bedroom as just a room to sleep in, but as a room with many different functions—working, watching television, reading. It can easily become an apartment within a house.

I think a television should be incorporated into the design of a room rather than hidden away, so I like to give it a pedestal. This X-shaped mahogany table has a slate top, which is almost indestructible.

Ask yourself certain questions. How do I want to feel when I open my eyes in the morning? How much storage do I need? How much reading light? A single person might need only one large night table, but a couple of bookworms would need two—and not necessarily matching ones. If the bed is elaborate, think of simplified night tables. If the bed is simple, balance it with an elaborate piece on one side, such as an eighteenth-century table, and a medium-size detailed piece on the other—one from the 1940s perhaps. If you need to do work in the bedroom, placing a desk near the bed with a nightstand on the other side gives the space the variety of two heights.

The television has a way of invading and pervading our environment, especially in the bedroom, but I never hide it. Unless they are very cleverly designed, television cabinets tend to look awkward and ungainly, and televisions today, especially the flat-screen versions, are not as aesthetically challenging as they used to be. For me, it is another piece of furniture, and you can play up its special physical character. Put a shiny, dark, slick set on a carved mahogany console, hide the wires, and suddenly you've got an interesting composition. And put the television where you have a clear line of sight without making it into an altar.

In so many houses and apartments, the bedroom is the only place where people can escape, the sole area where they allow themselves a bit of fantasy and drama. A bedroom has to perform the obvious functions, but it also has a much more fragile and ultimately psychological role. Somehow it is a woman's turf, a feminine boudoir rather than a masculine lair. So I usually slant the

bedroom more toward the woman. There is a sensual thing about entering a woman's bedroom. A man always likes to be invited in.

DRESSING THE BED I think of beds as boats that wrap you up and take you floating into dreams. I love white sheets, and I like to layer the bed. On a queen-size bed, I might use two twenty-six-inch-square European pillows, four standard pillows and two boudoir pillows. If I use pattern, it is subtle, and layered as well. I might use a row of European pillows in a tone-on-tone white damask, one row of standard pillows in a tiny overall pattern with a slight texture, and another row of standard pillows in damask. And finally, one row of boudoir pillows in a tiny overall pattern. I like a damask top sheet, perhaps with a merino wool blanket over it. I hate bedspreads. I prefer a comforter at the foot of the bed. You should always feel as if you can get into bed at any time. It should not be a chore to pull down the sheets. I love hospital corners. Having linens changed as often as possible is Nirvana to me. There is nothing like the feeling of slipping between freshly ironed sheets.

COLLECTIONS I never buy just one of an item, I buy at least three. Once I find something I love, I look for more examples everywhere. If you put just one thing on a shelf, it gets lost in the shuffle and becomes a lonely object. When I design a space for a client who collects, the first thing I do is group everything together. It may be 1950s glass, black-and-white portrait photography, or a big bowl of stones found on the beach and polished smooth by the waves. Displaying a collection together makes a much stronger statement than dispersing the pieces around a room. If you gather them into a group, they take on a physical presence. You notice all the objects; they earn your attention.

Once the items are assembled, I arrange them so that they play off each other. I'll juxtapose two traditional candlesticks with a modern one—the same kinds of objects but seen from the perspective of different periods. I position them with larger objects that are compatible in terms of color or shape. I am very careful about placement. If the pieces are small, such as Japanese netsukes, I put them at eye level, usually isolated from other things, to give them greater prominence. I like surprising displays. When you arrange things in new ways, you see them afresh. A collection of ivory will look very graphic inside a dark

A pile of crisp white pillows creates layers of softness on the bed. All the upholstery in the room is done in equally soft seashell colors. Remember that bedside tables don't have to match in style, age, or height. In fact, it's usually more interesting when they don't.

Rather than hanging these two photographs side by side, I stacked them to echo the verticality of the slim window. I liked the shape and patina of the Indian bronze holy water containers. In a way, they echo the lines of this nineteenth-century French oak country table.

OPPOSITE: In Calcutta, I chanced upon a collection of ivory boxes. Instead of buying just one or two, I bought them all. One is never enough.

teak cabinet. Any collection can be backlit to emphasize the silhouette of the shapes, whether you are featuring toy fire engines or Arts and Crafts pottery.

I once decorated a room that had a window with a great view at one end and a sofa at the other end, just sitting in front of a blank wall waiting for something above it. I could have chosen a painting, but I wanted something unpredictable. I brought out eight shovels that I had purchased at yard sales and flea markets throughout the country. No one would automatically think of hanging a shovel above a sofa, but even the most utilitarian object can be beautiful if you look at it with a fresh eye. Each shovel was carved out of one piece of wood, and the arched forms read clearly against the white wall. There was truth in quantity. If there had been only three, it would not have worked as well. I mounted them so that there was a rhythmic up-and-down movement to the group. The collection gave the wall weight, holding its own opposite the view. Taken out of their usual environment, the shovels became sculpture.

Price does not determine the visual value of any accessory, and mixing objects often elevates the stature of a piece. Take something from Pottery Barn and put it next to a magnificent Chinese vase; suddenly the plain and simple piece looks rather magnificent.

TABLESCAPES Just as I might balance a curvaceous sofa with a straight modernist chair, I create tablescapes by placing a polished, sophisticated object next to something naive. Diversity is the key—a delicate balance of different shapes, textures, scales, and provenance. As with a Japanese floral arrangement, make sure that you have something high, something medium, and something low. It is the play of one form against another that gives strength to the composition.

THE TRAVELING EYE When traveling, I don't look for the kinds of souvenirs you find in gift shops. Most of the time, little decorative souvenirs that were never used or loved by anyone won't survive the trip back to the United States; they don't make the cut. Instead I look at the objects people use every day—a wooden spoon, a water jug—and try to imagine them transplanted to another place. In India, for instance, I bought a collection of smooth stone lingams;

Hanging art or found objects are best left to professionals, who can execute your vision in the most unobtrusive way. Half the magic of this arrangement is that you don't see what's holding these shovels up. They look as if they were balanced right on top of the sofas.

PAGE 106: A red leather Chinese trunk holds an array of objects, from topiary to Thai bronze lime containers to Tibetan cookie molds. When composing one of these tabletop still lifes, I always aim for a range of heights.

PAGE 107: A tabletop collection of fourteenth-century Thai pottery is the focal point of a larger composition. Contemporary photography hangs alongside an eighteenth-century Swedish mirror, and the vaguely traditional fringed sofa is complemented by ebony-black webbed chairs I designed for Niedermaier. The client's son often sits here to practice his cello.

even out of their cultural context, their integrity is still intact. You do not need to know anything about their religious meaning to appreciate them as powerful objects. The same is true of a little leather-topped drum I once bought in Bhutan, or Indian cowbells, or wooden Japanese combs—objects that carry with them a strong sense of the culture from which they came.

Sometimes it is not what you buy but the things you find that ultimately give you the most pleasure. I frequently pocket a rock or a piece of wood for its color and texture. When I am in Thailand, I always try to go to the Sunday market in Bangkok. Outdoor markets are great places for the unexpected. I have found objects on blankets in the middle of the Himalayas that, when cleaned and polished, turn out to be things I treasure—betel nut boxes, turquoise and silver amulets. On one trip, I picked up bush ladders, carved stools, heavy metal bracelets used as currency, and hand-loomed fabrics for pillows. Remember to consider how a newfound treasure will integrate with the rest of your objects, and what it will say. I have accumulated a number of primitive blackwood snakes, with nicely carved and polished heads, that are as graphic and strong as any serious piece of sculpture. The secret to keeping your eyes open is to keep your life open to adventure.

The ceiling in this room is a soaring twenty feet high. To bring a more human scale to the space, I hung this eighteenth-century French boiserie panel just three inches above the sofa, to create a sense of intimacy.

PAGES 110 AND 111: When I was in Bhutan, I saw these people playing with small prayer drums and talked them into selling them to me. As part of the deal, I took a photograph to send back to them to show how an object can travel from the Himalayas to a New York coffee table.

color

From the moment I arrived in New York City, my big escape was going to museums. There was a time when I could tell you where every painting was hanging in the Metropolitan Museum of Art. That was the real beginning of my education. I was training myself aesthetically. Art for me was a process and a tool.

I was never a reader. The art museum was my book, and I would study the paintings to learn about composition and color. Standing in front of a van Gogh wheat field, I was struck by the power of the elemental. I could feel the sun and the wind, and with them an underlying thrill of tension and drama. I would stare at a delicate Indian miniature, and mentally pull out the colors the artist combined so deftly—lime-green, black, beige, orange, persimmon, gold. I responded immediately to Degas's subtle tonality—a blur of dark green, gray, taupe, white, and yellow, with touches of black; I have borrowed it many times and built rooms around his palette. Again and again I return to certain colors—caramel, beige, and creamy white, sea green or pale blue, dashes of black.

Taking up photography has changed the way I design. It has brought a new infusion of color into my rooms. Traveling with my camera has helped me see things differently; it has expanded my vision and refined my eye. Through a controlled aperture, you create a composition. It helps me look at everything else in a more concrete way. If I ever get tired and frustrated and my routine seems stale, all I have to do is jump on a plane. When I travel, I see things anew.

Whenever I go to Egypt, I feel as if I am traveling back in time. I met these Bedouins with their wares in the desert, which runs right up to the Nile.

A beautiful rug is like a piece of art. You don't have to match it, or pull colors out of it, when you're choosing upholstery. It can stand on its own. The brass lamps that flank either side of the sofa are like jewelry for the room; they bring a shimmer to the pale tones.

Setting off at five o'clock in the morning when it was still dark and jouncing in a Jeep through the Indian countryside outside of Rajasthan, I at first thought the desert was all one color, homogenous and bland. But then the sun broke, and as it rose, I looked through the lens and realized there was an amazing variety of color—not to mention an infinite array of browns. I always travel with little plastic bags, and when I see colors I like, I grab a sample. From this trip, I brought home a handful of sand, some sage-green brush, and a dark, weathered branch. I still have the branch for inspiration— I might lend it to my furniture refinisher and ask him to stain a particular chair that color.

You, too, can find your own point of view. If you are not sure of yourself and color seems a great mystery, choose an artist whose work you like. Stand in front of one particular painting and identify each of the colors to see how they work together. As a layman, you are borrowing the eye of a color expert. Adopt your favorite artists as mentors and take off from there. Picture a Mark Rothko painting in which bold colors bleed into one another and get their energy from the blur.

Creating a room is like making a painting. You have to add and subtract color, playing with solid blocks and pale washes of pigment—not only on the walls but in the materials—until the balance feels right. In Rothko's paintings, the layering of colors creates still other shades. The mistake most people make is to isolate each color. Don't confine yourself to one note. Explore the tonal possibilities of closely related shades. Aim for diversity within a limited range. I like colors that are not true—is it peach or pink or putty? If a color is subtle enough, it will change as the light shifts—a blue so evanescent that it almost evaporates. That is why those iridescent silks from Thailand and India are so mesmerizing. When you glance at a fabric from one angle, it looks red, and green from another. That elusive quality enriches a room.

The most interesting environments are mercurial. With color alone, you can create a subtle sense of movement in a room. You do not need a rainbow of colors to achieve the effect; all it takes is one. If, for example, you like blue, choose several different hues for the upholstery so you have a range of tones

from light to medium to dark. When you layer color this way, you can get a delicate rippling effect as the light shifts during the day.

I instinctively aim for a flow of color. I might go from blue-gray to gray-green to green-blue. Then the color you see is in a constant state of transition. In a sense, there really is no beginning or end to each hue.

Light, whether its source is the sun or a lamp, always acts on colors and alters them. When a room is washed in light, colors begin to blend. Blues start to look green and greens start to look blue. If you shuffle colors within the same space, the different shades make the mix richer and more complex because the hues play with and against each other. This is how to give a room chromatic depth.

An artist painting a landscape will try to capture the green of the grass, the brown of a tree branch, the blue of the sky. It was simple to take my palette straight from nature—the blue-greens of the ocean at Montauk, the multitude of beiges that make up sand, the sunbleached grays and charred blacks of driftwood. When you are alone on the beach and utterly relaxed, you can really start to look. Notice how sand changes when it gets wet. Suddenly all the subtle colors come out, just as when water washes over a stone. You may have to force yourself to see things abstractly, to focus on color, texture, shape. It is a different way of seeing than we are used to, an approach that artists have mastered. Try to see things not for what they are, but for what they might become if they were transposed to a different situation. When you walk on a beach, what makes you select one shell instead of another? Pay attention to your own spontaneous choices. I look at a client's makeup to see what tones she likes on her skin, so that we end up choosing colors that are flattering to her.

For a clue to the colors you like, open your closet door. What are the predominant tones in your wardrobe? Do you gravitate to neutrals such as cream, beige, and gray? Is black your basic uniform? Or are you attracted to bright, bold blues and vivid greens? You may think red is your favorite color, but how many red items do you actually own?

When coloring a room, you should always work with a range of tones to add depth to the space. Here the warm bronzes and woods are balanced by the cooler green tones in the mirror frame and the upholstery.

A color scheme can come from anywhere. Forget fanning through hundreds of color chips on a paint wand, wondering, "Do I like this, or that?" It is confusing and much too analytical. Instead, look at the ocean or a grove of trees. I have started with a chip of cerulean blue paint from the hallway of the Quisisana Hotel in Capri, a fragment of silk from Thailand, a scrap of paper found on a street in New York. It will always be something that sets off a strong emotional reaction, something that pulls me in. Absorb everything in your environment. Put yourself in places that open up your senses. Creativity comes from a place deep inside you. Follow your instincts, and you will find what you need.

A young husband and wife asked me to decorate their beach house, and I was trying to find a direction when I saw a Degas painting of dancers. There, on the canvas, were all the colors the wife liked—taupe, yellow, green, and white. Suddenly I had an image to work with. Keeping the painting in mind, I began to plan the colors for her rooms.

I wanted the walls to be white, in the tradition of summer houses around the world. The clarity of Degas's yellow was balanced by darker, earthy tones, and I decided that dark floors would ground the space. I found some classic rattan furniture and stained it dark brown, which gave it a richer and more elegant look. If you choose stain rather than paint as your source of color, it will have more depth. I added light natural upholstery and yellow and white accents, almost like sunshine sprinkling the room. My friend Dara had an old potting box that had spent many years on a farm. I hauled it out, had a bronze base made and turned it into a rustic coffee table, which I set in front of the fireplace. An L-shaped sofa made an intimate seating area in one corner, with a big round ottoman covered in suede to bring in the taupe. A pot of ivy on the table supplied the green note.

To balance the lightness of the living room, I turned the library on the opposite side of the foyer into a dark shell by spray painting the floor-to-ceiling bookcases brown. Accessories such as a fourteenth-century Burmese torso, Japanese boxes, Indonesian door carvings, English silver candlesticks, and Chinese jade bowls give each room a flavor of other cultures and times.

LEFT TO RIGHT: A Venetian gondola was the inspiration for the bed; with such a dramatic item as the centerpiece, you barely need anything else in the room. A blue-gray door I saw in Tunisia inspired the colors in a Fifth Avenue bedroom. This shade of blue works well with sunny yellow, and conveys a subliminal sense of the sunlit sky.

BENJAMIN MOORE
ICEBERG
2122-50

BENJAMIN MOORE
LEMON SORBET
2019-60

BENJAMIN MOORE
TAOS TAUPE
2111-40

BENJAMIN MOORE
SEA FOAM
2123-60

BENJAMIN MOORE
VICTORIAN LACE
2100-70

BENJAMIN MOORE
ELMIRA WHITE
HC-84

LEFT TO RIGHT: In a man's bedroom, taupe and blue are a very restful combination. Color can vary according to light. The dusty rose on these loggia walls in Italy changes color according to the angle and the amount of light. Lay out the colors and textures on the beach and they would blend right into the landscape. If you look closely at nature, you will always find inspiration.

OPPOSITE: The starting point of this Manhattan bedroom was the graphic zebra rug, which cued the ebonized wood floor and white wool upholstery on the Eero Saarinen womb chair.

BENJAMIN MOORE
MUSTANG
2111-30

BENJAMIN MOORE
LEMON SORBET
2019-60

BENJAMIN MOORE
CLASSIC BROWN
2109-10

BENJAMIN MOORE
ICEBERG
2122-50

OPPOSITE: A Degas painting was the inspiration for this palette of sunny yellow silk, mahogany-stained wicker, and mocha suede. I hung a grid of eight mirrors above the corner sofa to act as virtual windows and catch the light.

LEFT: The brown that serves as an accent in the living room becomes the overall color of the library.

RIGHT: A Venetian sofa is covered in the same fabric as the upholstered bed—another variation on the pale blue tone of the walls. Curtains rise all the way to the ceiling to soften the window wall.

BENJAMIN MOORE
MAGENTA
2077-10

BENJAMIN MOORE
CRYSTAL BLUE
2051-70

BENJAMIN MOORE
NORTH SEA GREEN
2053-30

WHITE IS RIGHT White is the most interesting color, or noncolor, I know. As the day progresses and the quality of the light changes, white can read from cool blue to pearl gray, from oatmeal to taupe. There are a thousand shades of pale.

Just as light acts on color, color acts on light. White walls take on a green cast when the incoming sunlight is filtered through the leaves of a tree outside the window. There is no such thing as pure, unadulterated white. Any white you choose will be affected by the color of the curtains, by the tones of the upholstery. Color and light are inseparable. No tone stands alone.

Contrary to what most people think, my rooms are not all white, but they all have the freshness and serenity of white. I take advantage of color, even if it is barely visible—the white might be perfumed with violet or tinged with pink or blue-gray, like a shadow on snow.

I prefer colors that practically dissolve into thin air, and when I paint a room white, or near white, it neutralizes the perimeter and erases the boundaries, expanding the space as if it were going on forever. White walls disappear, and you are left with what is most important—the people and the furnishings. The energy goes to the center of the room.

When you walk into a red room, you're immediately required to assume a certain attitude and energy. I keep returning to white because it is very peaceful. It doesn't require you to think, creating a sense of calm and emptiness even when a lot of furniture fills a room. I always use the same white paint, Benjamin Moore Super White, because if you find something that works, why change it?

I like to deal with old spaces in a contemporary way, and white can reinvigorate a room weighed down with elaborate moldings and plasterwork and cornices. If everything were painted beige, the room would start to get old again. You can wipe the slate clean with white and give a room a fresh start; it brings a sense of openness and clarity.

White is the great unifier, but it also sets off other shades and shapes so beautifully, which is why you often find it on the walls in art galleries.

PAGE 126: The house was originally built with a walk-in fireplace, which was never used. I turned it into a seating alcove and upholstered the walls, loose-back sofa, and club chairs in the same teal chenille. This color relates to the sky blue ribbed twill on the tight-back sofa and club chairs. The round frosted glass tabletop picks up the blue tones. The eclectic mix of furniture—a round 1950s table by Vidal Grau, a Chinese coffee table, gilded Italian chairs, an African stool—reflects the home owners' far-flung vision. Not everything matches, but it all works together.

PAGE 127: All the fabrics in the furnishings of this master bedroom are basically the same color, but different textures absorb the light differently, which creates a watery sheen.

OPPOSITE: My client's favorite color was pink. So why not go all the way with bubble-gum pink upholstery? You have to admit it really punches up the brown tones of the wood trim and the Aubusson rug.

I had a cigar in my hand when I was thinking about the palette in this room, so I decided to explore various tonalities of tobacco brown. A French chair stands next to a rusted iron table that dates from the time of the Eiffel Tower. The ottoman is one I designed for Niedermaier. A linen rug sits on the bleached floor. The bronze vessels are from India.

Furniture has a stronger presence in the surrounding bareness. Features read more clearly against a blank backdrop, especially if the white carries onto the floor—a bleached or pickled hardwood or a pale wall-to-wall carpet, for example. White puts pressure on the furniture to anchor the room and keep it from floating away, so you have to choose pieces with real character, or a sense of volume, so it won't all be too ethereal. If I use antiques, I arrange them in a contemporary way, profiling them against bare walls like art objects.

Sometimes I counter all the white with a bit of black, but just a touch, because black has a tendency to take over and overwhelm whatever is next to it. Black is like an exclamation point in a room; it can be used as an accent. It changes your focus. A black border on a rug delineates space; it snaps the room to attention. Black floors and white walls are very graphic. Black can make a space look so modern.

NEUTRALS Our concept of neutrals has changed. When designers did a neutral room back in the 1970s, everything was the same beige. Now a neutral room will run the gamut from off-white to dark cement. Instead of just one color, there will be many different tones: hemp, taupe, almond, parchment. I am always trying to duplicate the warm tones of sand when it's wet, or the color of the bark on a pine tree. I don't even like calling them neutrals, which makes them sound blah and boring. I think of them as naturals. They are earth tones. I relax when I use them because they make me feel closer to nature. It is a subliminal association, but a very strong one because I feel connected to the outdoors. It is the foundation for creating a warm, inviting environment.

Natural tones have a way of grounding a room, and I might use the two noncolors, black and white, as accents. White brings out the softness of the earth tones, and black creates a sharp, sophisticated contrast. Interestingly, you can get all sorts of effects in the same room just by adding different accents. When you put a pink next to a neutral, suddenly you can see tones of pink in it. Put a green next to it and it takes on a greenish cast. This flexibility is wonderful, and it explains why natural colors have such longevity. You can transform a space without changing everything in the room. More and more,

BENJAMIN MOORE
SMOLDERING RED
2007-10

BENJAMIN MOORE
CHILI PEPPER
2004-20

I am using neutrals that have a tint to them, for instance a greenish-taupe or a pinkish-beige. When you consider neutrals, don't see them as just one color, but as a rainbow of possible effects.

DARE TO GO DARK When you start thinking about dark colors, you have to be aware of your skin and hair tones and what will be flattering to them. If you have sallow skin, you don't want to paint your room dark green. If you are blond, you would look better in a dark brown room than in a red one. But if you have black hair, red would be a wonderful backdrop. When I think of dark colors, I think of jewels. What is it about rubies, emeralds, and sapphires that makes them so appealing? It usually has to do with the depth of color. You can get a similar kind of depth in a room by upholstering the walls in iridescent silk, doing a crosshatch glaze in two tones of burgundy, or by just using high-gloss paint in a color such as emerald green. It is actually very soothing to be engulfed in deep, saturated color. When you work with dark colors, it can be very dangerous to use flat paint. Often it becomes very chalky and absorbs all the light instead of reflecting it, which creates a sense of mustiness and age. I would rather play against the darkness and make the paint reflective and shimmering, so you turn the negative into a positive.

I see rooms as introverted or extroverted. For me, a library or study is the type of introverted space where I might use an intense color such as bottle green or a dark, moody slate blue. That is especially true now that computer screens require dimmed light rather than blasts of sun. Dark colors also work well in a dining room, imparting intimacy and warmth while enhancing the flicker of candlelight and the sheen of silver. A powder room can acquire a sense of drama if it is painted garnet red or sapphire blue. But you have to be fully committed when you do a dark room. A shade that is not quite light and not quite dark can end up looking muddy.

Don't make the mistake of picking out one hue and trying to match everything too closely. You always want two or three shades of the same color running through walls, carpet, and upholstery to give a room some depth.

Red on red on red was the theme for this library. I painted the walls in a crosshatch strié using two shades of red. The leather sofa picks up the color, and I chose a rug to match. The gouache is by Fernand Léger.

You can think of a room in terms of poetry. In a conventional room, all the elements tend to rhyme. The sofa matches the rug that matches the walls. If you have an indigo and beige rug, the rhymer's impulse would be to pick up the indigo here and the beige everywhere else. I wouldn't do that. I prefer a kind of assonance, more like free verse.

PATTERN When choosing fabric, I rarely pick prints. For me, there is already enough pattern in the juxtaposition of colors as you enter a room. I find that printed fabrics freeze the color combinations instead of allowing that subtle shift of shades that lends a room so much animation and life.

A printed fabric is a type of applied decoration. It distracts you from the pure shape of a piece of furniture. You notice the print first. I would rather focus attention on what is integral to the piece, such as the curve of a leg or the slant of a seat. Pattern isolates the individual piece in space. Color integrates a piece of furniture into its surroundings.

Just because there are no printed fabrics on the chairs doesn't mean there is no pattern in my rooms. I prefer to find my pattern in other, more unexpected places. In this living room, a collection of Beaux-Arts architectural details—plaster models once studied and sketched by Parisian students—hangs on a wall. It's a piecemeal architectural frieze that functions as a work of art.

light

At one point we lived in a rooftop apartment in Cuba with windows on all four sides, and from every window there was a different view of the city and the harbor of Havana. I can still close my eyes and see Morro Castle and the ocean. My mother always put up curtains in our other houses, but this time she never got around to it. That pure, unobstructed view was so much more beautiful than any pair of curtains. This was where I first began to understand the importance of light.

I think of light as a construction, and building light starts at the window with the sun. When I am beginning a design, I visit the space on a bright day to see just how light enters. I am there early in the morning, at midday, and again late in the afternoon as the sun is setting, to feel the quantity and quality of the light.

If you choose to put nothing on the windows, the shapes of the windows themselves will be repeated on the floor. For a long time, I was a big supporter of large, uninterrupted expanses of glass, but now I like the grids you get with paned windows. You see the shadow of the mullions projected by the sun, and the squares give the space a different dimension and a traditional feel. Gridded windows can break up an unfortunate view, and like the cracks of light you see through a slatted fence or the shadows it casts onto a road, the patterns give a room visual character. I think about how the light will play on the floor, and the feeling that it will create.

Located on the funky canals of Venice, California, this house with its two-story window wall was bombarded by photons, as though it were in the Caribbean. Though bright, the quality of light was fragile because it was in constant motion, shimmering on the surface of the water and reflecting up into the interiors. With a long run of translucent cotton curtains, I captured and transformed the light ricocheting through the windows. In direct sun, the wall of curtains glows like a bulb, bathing the living room in soft light.

LEFT: Light creates its own patterns. A wavy bamboo fence is reproduced in shadow on a roadside in Bhutan.

RIGHT: As the sun strikes a Moroccan window, it projects the grid.

OPPOSITE: In this living room with a view of the Atlantic Ocean, venetian blinds filter the light while making their own graphic statement.

Venetian blinds, so practical for controlling the sun on south-facing windows, pattern the surfaces of a room in the same way, creating a graphic landscape of stripes that climbs up furniture and crosses pillows. Those shadowy striations make you feel as if you have stepped into a 1940s movie. Equally cinematic is the traveling cone of light that streams through a skylight: It describes the path of the sun on the floor like a sundial marking time.

You get an entirely different effect with frosted glass, practical and beautiful for different reasons: The foggy surface diffuses light, taking off the edge. Shadows on its misty surfaces blur, as on shoji screens, making the daily dance of light and shade more subtle. Of course, you have to keep things simple inside so that the nuances will register.

When you understand how the natural light coming into a room behaves, you can begin to think about what sort of window treatments would be appropriate and how to balance natural and artificial light. If you like a bright, sunny space, all you really need is a gauzy scrim that veils a window. Like frosted glass, it cuts the glare and softens the shadow and the view, giving a sense of romance and privacy. The light is filtered, as though it were coming through translucent leaves in a forest. If you look at Impressionist paintings, such as summer scenes painted by Manet or Renoir, the colors seem to quiver and blur, as if seen through a haze. Filtered light allows tonalities to blend rather than separate. A gauzy window covering evens out the light and tempers the edge of the reality outside by blurring the details, imparting a dreamlike quality. Window treatments are certainly an element you can use to create a certain emotion.

I automatically gravitate toward a full-blast southern exposure. Maybe it's the Cuban in me—I love sitting there, squinting. If the light is too bright, I use a lined shade to lower the intensity. Curtains offer another layer of protection and add softness to a space. A pale blue fabric for the shades creates the sense of a blue sky outside, even on cloudy days. It fools the eye. But I don't use heavy fabric panels or elaborate swags around a window casing. Often they smother light. I think the more natural light there is, the better.

PAGE 142: In Taos, New Mexico, gauzy cotton shades soften the blinding natural light. A pair of mattresses upholstered in sage-colored chenille doubles as guest beds. Pillows pick up the shade of the adobe walls.

PAGE 143: Bright yellow shades and pale yellow walls bring the sun into this Long Island bedroom, even on a cloudy day.

For a fellow Cuban living in Venice, California, I created the essence of a Spanish courtyard with an iron gate, potted jasmine, and a trickling fountain.

LEFT: Thick walls in hot climates provide shelter from the light and keep a room cool.

RIGHT: A traditional gilded French sconce lights up a corner when the sun goes down.

OPPOSITE: Wall-to-wall linen gauze filters the light while allowing the pattern of the windows to come through.

Light will affect colors during the course of a day. As light floods in, colors bleach out, and as colors fade, they start to merge. When the light outside dims, the colors come out again. Light is the catalyst for color's evolution. It is one of the elements I use to encourage the vaporous, changeable hues I love.

The degree of luminosity entering the windows dictates what you choose colorwise in the room. A sunny yellow or delicate blue will compensate for darkness in a room and help create the feeling of being outside. If a room is predominantly white, it elevates the intensity of the light. A room in shadows benefits from a single white wall, which bounces what light there is. (If a room is already bright, it will augment the light.) But sometimes you decide to go with the light that's available. If a room is dark, you may want to accentuate the intimacy with a deep, rich color.

I never use a colored scrim that tints the light at the window. That shifts the spectrum inside, and you always have to adjust it—it's like painting with sunglasses on. Scrims that are a plain, pure white clarify the colors inside, and when the sun strikes the material, the shades glow.

Natural light is transitory, changing with clouds and the time of day, so you have to create a core of artificial lighting that complements natural light when it is there and compensates when it is not. After sunset, it's a different ball game. Remember that a window becomes a black hole at night. You can draw the curtains or light it from outside if you want a continuity of light.

The function of a space—reading, computing, dining, sleeping—determines what kind of light you will need and where. Never do an electrical plan before you have finalized the furniture layout. You want to make sure you have outlets in all the right places, and perhaps a floor outlet or two to help eliminate trailing wires. Most rooms have multiple functions, which will require several kinds of lighting, from general ambient light to task lighting to accents. But solving the functional problems does not automatically lead to the solutions that gratify the eye and the soul. Many people automatically put the sofa in front of a window when they are arranging their living room. Think again—you may want to be sitting in the darker area of the room and

Black-shaded Hansen lamps provide good reading light as well as good design in this guest bedroom. Instead of designing two separate headboards, I decided to treat them as a single line, extending to each window. That gives the bed a greater architectural presence in a room that was basically a box.

looking at the light. It is more pleasant to look out the window than to sit with it at your back.

I think of a space as a stage on which the right lighting will create a mood, even without furnishings. The lighting scheme is not a secondary thought but a primary concern, and the idea is to be emotional instead of clinical, subjective rather than objective. The psychology of a space starts at the window because that is where you begin to handle the most basic element of a room, the light.

Evenness in lighting only makes a room look generic. Without focus and accent, all the details of a room cancel each other out. The hierarchy of parts melts into an undifferentiated field and the space loses its impact. In a room that works like a good stage set, the lighting brings out key players and marginalizes the supporting cast. If every corner is lit equally, the emphatic pieces meld into the surroundings, and the room goes flat.

It is like photographing a face: You need to light it the right way in order to show its best features. You apply the right makeup, highlighting certain parts while playing down other parts. Still, the total effect should come across as natural, not forced. A space that has a contrast of light and dark areas usually works well because dark corners in a room bring out the brightness, and the gradations of light add greater depth. Besides, the contrast of light and dark areas gives people a choice—they can find a seat to suit their mood.

Lighting automatically differentiates the parts of a space. You might position a spotlight to illuminate a table that will hold flowers, and then provide wall washers for the paintings. Just make sure some lights are low. Overhead lights can be harsh; lights that flatter a bouquet may not do the same for a face.

I use light to reveal texture, accentuate objects, create patterns, and give depth to a room. I use it to clarify and I use it to cheat. I can't think of another design element that can modify the mood of a room quicker than lighting. Just turn on the table lamps, and their glow will infuse the space with warmth. Halogens give a more intense, controlled light, very close to the sun in visual temperature. I never use fluorescents—life is already harsh enough. They

LEFT: A ray of sun highlights a pew in a Brazilian church.

RIGHT: Recessed lighting in the ceiling of this Manhattan bedroom creates a warm glow. The deeply inviting bed was inspired by a wing chair. Creamy silk curtains practically cocoon the room and camouflage an awkward layout, as well. The upholstered screen behind the bed adds a contrasting note.

change the overall color of a room, shifting it toward green. Incandescents can be too yellow, which also distorts colors. Generally it is best to keep the color of light as close to natural as possible. If you want to accentuate the sheen of lush silk curtains, you can place uplights on the floor. And don't forget old-fashioned candlelight for a touch of drama. With many light sources in different places, you can adjust the lighting pattern, bringing it to a balance that reduces the contrasts that create glare.

Light is architecture; it can reinforce a room's structure. Its patterns can play into and reinforce the composition and organization of a room—the symmetries, the placement of doorways, the proportions. A shot of light on a coffee table not only brings out its grain but creates a sense of place. Pooling light denotes sections of the room and manipulates space. Hansen lamps hung on a wall can bracket a sofa in light and create a secondary height below the ceiling, giving the space another, more intimate scale. This simple strategy creates a virtual alcove within the room.

If you want to raise the height of a ceiling or just enjoy its full span, use cove lighting. I like to place shaded sconces down hallways. Seen in a row, they have the regular rhythm of a colonnade. Lighting can bring out architectural features, but lights can also be the features themselves.

I hate bare lightbulbs, so when I am not interested in a fixture and I have the budget, I use recessed lighting on a dimmer. It gives you the flexibility to manipulate a room like a stage. You can light a room from above or from the sides, orchestrating the parts, bringing out the full depth of the space. For record producer Clive Davis, the stage is a second home. In his new guesthouse in upstate New York, I wanted to dramatize, subtly, the way the angled living room ceiling brought the trees inside. With the upturned roof planes opening up the interior, the living room and the exposed kitchen seemed like a sophisticated camp set outside in the woods under a tent. I treated the spaces like the thrust stage of a theater in the round. I did everything to invite the forest and its light into the space and to emphasize the interior's connection to the elements. The lacquered ceiling seems to float in its own reflection of the trees; its watery surface recalls the ponds painted by Monet.

LEFT: In a monastery in Ecuador, the sun streams through a courtyard loggia and, with light alone, duplicates the arches on the opposite wall.

RIGHT: An antique theatrical spotlight throws a pool of brightness on a tea table. It is interesting to see a hard-edged industrial object in this context. Just because a home is in the Southwest doesn't mean it has to be filled with Southwestern furnishings. A seventeenth-century French sofa, Chinese chairs, and a table I designed don't look out of place against the adobe walls.

PAGE 154: In the center of a kitchen island, a lamp rises from the floor and goes through the tabletop. Inspired by architects' lamps, the fixture has white frosted glass shades that adjust according to the task. A gilded deco chair mingles with casual wicker and a banquette at the other table.

PAGE 155: Firelight flickers off the copper-lined firebox. The mahogany above the mantel is polished to a high, reflective sheen. Standing behind the chaise is a simple and beautiful silver-plated standing lamp by Agostini, an Italian designer of the 1940s.

OPPOSITE: A stone floor laid in the same rough pattern as the walk outside blurs the boundaries between inside and out in this living room. The wall behind the sofa opens to an unseen interior stairwell, clad in the same clapboard as the exterior and topped by a clerestory window to let in more light.

The architect Mark Rios put a lot of energy into the roof, and I kept the ceiling free of light fixtures so the eye would glide up the wings, uninterrupted, and take off into the treetops. Even recessed lighting would have cut into the illusion of the floating ceiling. The tall wraparound windows made the room a bowl of light during the day, but of course we still had to have lighting. I hung custom-made bronze computerized theatrical lights on nickel-finish rods, off-stage. The soft metals take the hard edge off the fixtures, and the blinders give them the sense of fluttering. The kitchen is also located under one of the flying roof planes, so I designed a three-headed adjustable light attached to the stainless-steel worktop for the task lighting needed for cooking. The big, wide planes of glass that compose the house looked stunning during the day, but turned into dark, depressing voids at night. So I deployed spotlights among the trees outside. The blackness simply vanishes as the landscaping reappears with the help of a rheostat. Even at night you can bring out the connection between the outside and inside.

I grounded the living room with a flamed Chinese granite floor, earth-toned fabrics, and a Tabriz rug to emphasize the continuity with the woods outside, and I used table and floor lamps to create a zone of intimacy in the lofty space. The incandescent bulbs bring out the warmth of the natural colors. A Noguchi table lantern, with its rice paper shade, lends informality to the lighting scheme. I conceived the space as a landscape of loosely configured furniture. The lamps simply fell where they were needed, without any geometric plan. But you can choose to structure space with lights, and in the staircase I arranged a row of regularly spaced votive candles on small, simple bronze sconces that I designed. The lacquered wall reflects the flicker. In this tall, relaxed interior, the small sconces are unexpected, a yardstick of light measuring space in a dappled world.

LAMPSHADES When selecting a shade for a lamp, there are several decisions to be made. Do I want to follow the lines of the base or set up a contrast? Do I want a modern shade in some newfangled material or a classic shape in paper or silk? Should it register as a color itself or be utterly translucent?

I use a paper shade when I want to create a very concentrated pool of light, and I always choose a glossy finish to give the lamp a modern quality. If you use translucent silk, remember that the metal frame will show through, so think of having the silk shirred to obscure it or else play up the transparency by making the frame part of the design. I love parchment shades, and real goatskin because of its natural irregularities and the mottled quality of the light that comes through. In a bedroom, I might line a bedside lamp in pink silk to flatter skin tones.

Figuring out the size and color of lampshades is one of the hardest things to do. You need to try different shades with the lamp base. First, you have to determine the correct scale. There's no formula; it is all by the eye. But make sure the bottom of the shade comes down to the top of the base, like a capital on a column. I don't like seeing any part of the rod.

Next comes the question of shape and color. Decide whether you want to call attention to the lamp or make it an unobtrusive form within the environment. If it is going to be a decorative object, you can add trim or pattern or color. If you want it to disappear, stick with a simple white shade. Sometimes I trim an off-white lampshade in the same color as the walls, to bring the color into the center of the room. In a dark green library, I might choose dark green shades so they virtually disappear and you just see the light coming out of the bottom.

A shirred silk shade hangs from a brushed nickel rod over a stone table in a house in the Hamptons. The shade is large enough to balance the highly carved legs of the massive table, and the shirring lends a soft quality that suits a beach house. A wall-sized mirror doubles the light.

texture

A prospective client once told me, "Look at my room. There are all these fabrics on all this furniture, but it's dead." He was right—there was no point of view. The mistake a lot of people make is to isolate materials—to see them as single, stand-alone items in what amounts to a showroom. You have to understand that a room is like a canvas, not just one brushstroke in a corner but a tableau of brushstrokes, all of them related. So when you isolate a material on a wall or a sofa or a chair, you are starting to pull the canvas apart.

When I lay out materials in a space, I think in terms of the whole room, floor to ceiling, front to back. I try to visualize it in my mind's eye the way people would see it when they first walk in. And I always conceive it as a tactile composition.

I start at the perimeter, working my way in toward the middle, always playing one material and texture against another. The contrasts provoke interest. I am layering and creating a sense of depth in a space through differentiation. Nothing makes a fabric or a material look smoother than to put it against something rough. If the curtains are silk, I might put a ribbed cotton on the sofa and leather on the ottoman. I always tell clients not to think of any one finish as the only finish, but to have several and juxtapose them in the way you would group antiques with more contemporary furniture. A gilt chair next to an African stool works in the same way as silken sheen next to a matte waxed surface. That idea applies as much to fabrics and materials as it does to shapes, colors, and furniture types.

A collection of objects sits on a woven tray on a rattan ottoman. I like layering one rectangular shape on top of another, and then the boxes add a whole other element. The sheen of the intricately inlaid silver is a nice contrast to the straw.

I like wood in all its infinite variations. A painted and gilded Swedish chair stands next to a French oak table, in front of a slatted teak screen. I designed the mahogany lamp. Propped alongside is an Indian reverse painting on glass.

PAGE 166: The contrast of black leather and white silk pillows is a surprise, but a pleasing one. The sofa is upholstered in wool bouclé from VW Home. I brought in more texture with the pickled oak table resting on a bronze frame. The ottoman is tufted leather.

PAGE 167: Texture seduces the eye and makes even the simplest interior intriguing. Each one of these objects can stand up to repeated scrutiny—a Chinese lattice window, an African ladder, a ribbed oak lamp on a Chinese table. Both the leather ottoman and the gilded 1940s chair look just fine standing on a poured concrete floor.

I love blending various woods—light, dark, lime-rubbed—in a space. Different woods can exist in your room just as they do in the forest. It's like cooking: You don't add all ingredients in the same quantity. Some are strong spices that you use sparingly for a little kick, and others you can wield more generously. But the binder for it all should be a cohesive thought or overarching idea traveling through the space.

If it's a bedroom, you might want to express sensuality and eliminate any sharpness or hardness. Do you want a restful space? Do you want this room to have a womblike quality? Putting fabric on the walls is one way to achieve a sensual bedroom. It muffles sound and gives it a sense of isolation within the house; a couple will be able to feel alone there together. But do you want the softness to be expressed in a fabric with a sheen or with a pronounced texture? If you decide on a textured fabric, a cut-pile carpet on the floor will set off the walls. If the wall fabric has a sheen, then the floors should have the texture.

A sense of place might be the driving idea in a room. If you want a field or lawn outside to come visually into the living room, choosing the right materials is a good place to begin. It could be as simple as bringing the stone (which is usually rough, to prevent slipping in the rain) from an adjacent patio indoors, to establish visual continuity. But should the rough texture carry through with a stone loosely set in a naturalistic pattern? (Appropriate for a country house. Think Frank Lloyd Wright and his organic approach to materials.) Or should it be done with a smoother, more strictly laid stone that tells something about how interiors domesticate the idea of nature? (Suitable for a modern house. Think how Mies van der Rohe refined rough edges.) You could go either way. You might also lacquer the walls to capture the trees outside in a shimmering reflection.

Of course, the choice of a material has to be practical. The flooring in a high-traffic entry hall or kitchen should be durable, and you don't want to fall in the bathroom because you used slippery wall tiles on the floor. But within the range of what is practical, you should think about the materials that give you pleasure—silk, wool, sisal, suede—and rank them in your mind. Start blending them in a hypothetical design to imagine to what degree you'd like to use

each. Will the sheen cover the whole sofa or just the pillow on the sofa? If a banquette or chaise longue is smooth, maybe the club chairs nearby are textured. This is true not just for fabrics, but also for woods, stones, and metals. If you decide to cover the sofa in a smooth silk with a sheen, you may want a table with a stone top on brushed metal legs that is not as shiny, or a wonderful piece of wood, on a statuary bronze base, for the top.

The Italian architect Gio Ponte said, "Nothing exists if not through the hands." When a house offers a cashmere throw or a cool tablet of marble to our fingers, it is giving the gift of texture. When we reach out for a seashell or a piece of driftwood on a mantelpiece, we are breaking through the bell jar that more and more seems to surround and separate us from the physical world. We are making personal contact with a house: It is like touching the arm of a friend in a sensitive moment. Twisting a solid door handle, lifting a hefty brass knocker, or turning a heavy faucet amounts to shaking a house's hand, and we judge the building—even the occupant and the designer—by the character of the touch.

There is something real about a house in which textures flourish. In a world that seems to exist increasingly on screen, beyond our grasp, the house full of tactile surfaces invites our touch and grounds us. It's a refuge for our senses. Even a simple, waxed pine table or a sisal carpet can refresh us when we graze it with our fingers or take off our shoes. The skin comes alive with a little traction. And the textures send messages; they often refer to a larger order beyond domestic space. A wide-board softwood floor cues thoughts of lumber and forests. We are understanding a basic, more elemental world through our fingers: When we touch, we wonder.

Sometimes texture goes hand in hand with the choice of furniture, and if you mix the furniture you mix the textures. I have used wicker chairs, a banquette, and a deco armchair around the same slate dining table. The weave of the wicker contrasts with the plush forms of the banquette, upholstered in chenille. And that sets off the smooth wool of the armchair, with its frame highlighted in gold.

Walls striéd in three shades of blue give this library a dark, inky tone that sets off the lime-rubbed oak etagere. Pale linen on the chair frames adds another texture, and offers a delicate contrast to the dark leather seats. The painting is by Damian Loeb.

Ebonized brick floors and adobe walls suggest the patina of age in a brand-new house. A bleached tree trunk becomes a pillar, and the round wooden beams are a further reminder of nature. Old Mexican hammered tin sconces flank a limestone fireplace. A weathered Swedish clock presides over the dining area.

Texture is character, and it elicits different responses. You sit on an elegant silk differently than you do on a more casual chenille. Leather and suede are like plaster is to a sculptor—they allow you to define and accentuate the forms of the furniture. Natural linen is indestructible; it has an inherent ease and brings an earthiness to the space. I love the rich colors of silk and the mottled blur of linen velvet, which comes off the bolt already looking old.

Sometimes I upholster the walls of a bedroom or a library in wool or leather. You sense the softness just by looking at it. The added texture gives the room a particular warmth that makes it feel more intimate. Texture humanizes the environment. We go to the country to refresh ourselves with an immersion in things that are raw to the touch—rough woods, green grass, worn stone. The primitive in us is still alive if we just remind our nerve endings.

DOORKNOBS It is very important to know when you want to see a doorknob, and when you don't. On a front door, which I always paint black, I use a traditional brass doorknob to convey a sense of the past. If the interior doors are solid wood, with raised panels, I like to use a classic doorknob, especially a large one with a sculptural quality. I like the way an egg-shaped doorknob feels in my hand. A doorknob can be a design statement if you go beyond the generic. On the other hand, you want the hardware to disappear on a flush door designed to form a continuous plane with the surrounding wall. A prominent handle would break the illusion.

HINGES In a modern space, I like to use satin nickel hinges, but if it's a more traditional environment, I opt for brass. A yellow metal implies older buildings, a white metal suggests a more contemporary edge. Many people feel if they use satin nickel in one place, then everything has to be satin nickel. But just as you might wear a gold bracelet and a stainless-steel Rolex watch at the same time, you can put a brass doorknob on a door with nickel hinges. If it all matches, the element you're trying to highlight loses its impact. If you want the focus to be on the doorknob, try mixing metals. Break some rules.

Pale green–lacquered walls set off a traditional truffled limestone floor in the elevator foyer of a Manhattan apartment. The 1940s light fixture is made of plaster. The sculpture is by Eric Fischl.

PERSONAL BEST: MATERIALS

I find myself coming back to certain materials again and again. I love:

- Limestone, because it brings a natural lightness to the shell of a space, without any pattern and because it is functional. Crab orchard stone, which I often use on floors, has a great texture and color: it runs from camel to taupe to cream, and can have a lovely pink tone.

- Leather, because it is the closest thing to skin and a comforting material, especially if it's aniline-dyed (a very high-quality dye that goes all the way through the hide). The more banged up and worn it is, the more special leather becomes. I like to juxtapose it with suede because they are the same elements, but seen in two different ways— smooth and textured.

- Polished wool, which is smooth like billiard cloth, because it gives a structured architectural feeling to furniture and a modernist cachet to antiques.

- Thai silk, because it brings texture and light to a space with its watery tonalities. The woven silk thread takes the dye in different ways, so there is a lot of variation to it.

- Linen, which is one of the oldest fabrics known to man, for its imperfections and the softness it takes on with time. The fact that it has wrinkles, just as we do, is somehow very comforting.

- Linen velvets, because of their sheen and shadings. As you walk by a piece of furniture upholstered in it, the colors change.

- Chenille, because of its softness. Its long nap creates a broad range of tonalities.

- Sheer wool for curtains, because of the way it hangs: It has enough body to fold and drape beautifully.

- Lime-rubbed wood, because, with two tones of white and natural wood color within the same piece, it's a way of getting light and depth. The grain shows up beautifully.

- Teak, which is a very hard wood from Asia, looks best when it's left unsealed. It gets a lovely aged patina and turns a very warm color. Teak floors are beautiful.

- Sapele mahogany for its longitudinal grain that ripples as you move around it. Mahogany in general, because it's a beautiful wood that comes in so many tones. It always adds distinction to a space, and contrasts so dramatically with pale woods and fabrics.

- Ebony, for its blackness.

- Low-pile Italian wool carpet in solid colors, because it is a luxurious, low-key way to wrap a space.

home

I live on the edge of Manhattan, in a gritty neighborhood of parking garages and bus terminals just west of the Garment District. I found a loft with big old industrial windows on the eleventh floor of an anonymous 1920s office building and moved in when few people would consider living in this no-man's-land. But I didn't mind the grit, and I loved the wide-open space washed with light. Recently, I bought the loft next door and combined the two spaces, which meant I had the opportunity to redesign.

Working for myself is the easiest job. I'm not demanding, I'm not indecisive, and I always agree with myself. There are no expectations. I'm allowed to think freely, and the only one I have to answer to concerning the budget is me.

In redesigning, there were certain givens. I think a residential loft should still show its industrial roots, so I didn't try to hide the pipes and sprinklers. That raw quality is exactly what makes a loft special; in fact, if a loft is too polished, I think you're cheating yourself. I personally don't need to have a perfect space. I don't have to buy top-of-the-line appliances, or obsess over the paint job. Those things are not important to me. What I do care about is light, views, and space.

I like the simple architectural lines of this eighteenth-century Swedish table as well as its flexibility. I can fold it down so it practically disappears, or open it up for dining. Against one wall is a parade of chairs, near enough to pull around the table for a party. I let guests select their own chairs, to suit their personality. Photographs are propped everywhere because I hate pinning them down. I want people to be able to pick them up for a closer look. I treat my apartment as a gallery, and I'm always rearranging my collections into new groupings.

In an unconventional space, I wanted an unconventional arrangement of furniture. The elegant Louis XVI gilded bench and nineteenth-century Russian chair rub shoulders with a purely fake trompe-l'oeil drum. All the pieces can move around at a whim. I designed the sofa and club chairs gathered around the Giacometti-esque coffee table. The cement floors are finished in Benjamin Moore Super White deck paint and are so reflective that they give the sense that the whole room is floating.

PAGE 182: A series of Robert Longo drawings on vellum hangs above a 1940s French limed-oak pool chaise that I use as an ottoman. Just beyond is the guest room, where the television rests on an industrial forklift.

PAGE 183: The guest room sofa doubles as a bed when sheets are spread over the upholstered mattress. A stark steel frame supports the pillows and plays on the grid of the windows. I took the photograph hanging on the wall in Sikkim.

The loft measures three thousand square feet, with four exposures. On one wall is a glorious run of twelve windows facing south. You can't beat the drama of seeing a dozen windows in a row, and I didn't want to interrupt that stretch, but when you've got such a long expanse, you need something to bracket it. So I built slim shelves at either end to show off my own photography and a collection of photographs by others.

To play up the sense of space, I kept the plan open, rather than breaking up the loft into neat little rooms. Only the bedroom and bath have sliding doors for privacy. The walls, ceilings, and floors are all painted white for continuity. There are no window treatments, nothing to interfere with the view. Instead of a conventional seating arrangement in the living area, with two chairs facing a sofa, I decided to let the furniture float. I wasn't thinking about ensembles or trying to fit everything into a preconceived format. I just treated each chair like a piece of sculpture and set it wherever I wanted. It feels as if it all fell into place. I can pull a few chairs together if friends come over, and it doesn't matter if I put them back in a totally different spot. It's a very forgiving environment.

All the furniture means something to me. There are pieces I found on my travels and bought to sell, but somehow I couldn't part with them. The sofa belonged to a friend who didn't want it anymore. Each piece has its own personality, and when you put them next to each other, it's like spices in a bouillabaisse. The flavor gets more complex.

I don't do much cooking in the city, so I didn't want to devote a lot of space to the kitchen. I just wanted something that would be functional and inexpensive and easy to maintain, so I chose simple white Formica counters and cabinets. I like them because they disappear.

The bathroom is my one real luxury. I've always wanted a huge, freestanding shower, so I designed a room with a shower head in the ceiling. An eight-foot-square section of the floor beneath is sunken. For a vanity, I used a beautiful dark wood table that I found in Thailand, and put a sink on top that looks like a bowl. An old silver goblet holds my toothbrush, and there are always fresh

PAGE 184: Picture ledges at either end of this library hall display my photography collection. A 1950s bronze Italian table stands in front of the frosted glass wall that separates the library and the master bath.

PAGE 185: I love orchids and I'm always rescuing abandoned plants. I keep them in the bedroom because I like to wake up with the blooms. The first thing I do every morning is check to see if any stalks are sending up new buds. At first I thought I'd get an industrial steel table for them, but I decided it was much more intriguing to set the simple clay pots on this extravagant eighteenth-century Italian console.

OPPOSITE: I put the bed in the center of the master bedroom and designed a freestanding wall to create a sense of shelter. Because it doesn't touch the ceiling or the other walls, you don't feel boxed in. The photograph by Edward Munkacsi is hung asymmetrically, which is much more interesting than if it were centered.

OPPOSITE: As you enter the master bath, you see a Burmese table holding a stainless-steel sink shaped like a bowl. It feels like a piece of furniture rather than a fixture.

LEFT: It's a pleasure to stand in the center of this room and have water hit you from all sides. The limestone shower is bathed in natural light filtering through the frosted glass, which gives the room a mystical quality. Objects on the other side create mysterious shadows.

RIGHT: In a niche in the shower, an Indian marble window stands in front of a frosted glass panel. I like to bring the exotic into the realm of everyday life.

flowers or an orchid plant nearby. None of the furniture looks like bathroom furniture; it feels more like a "real" room. Two of the walls are covered in marble and the others are frosted glass, letting the light from the windows come through. All the light fixtures are on dimmers, so I can control the mood. The bathroom is open to the bedroom; I can close it off with a sliding door.

The loft is my retreat. I have done exactly what I wanted to the space and filled it with objects I love in the casual way I want to live. You, too, can take your space into your own hands. I'm not suggesting you copy what I've done, because the point is not to mimic anyone but to follow your own muse, whether you choose a designer or design yourself. What I am offering is a template—a few strategies to adopt or discard to get you started—because once you have really learned to see, you will find what you like and go your own way. Designing anything is a process, and you should continue to add and subtract. Change is what keeps a space, and an individual, alive. How do you want to feel when you walk into a room? Comfortable? Tranquil? Energized? Once you know what makes you feel good, you can create a room that reflects your own emotions and sensibility. Designing is all about getting in touch with yourself.

FLOWERS Flowers make a space seem suddenly fresh and clean. I love yellow flowers—they bring a sense of sunshine to a room. But when in doubt, white is always a good choice. I like a bouquet to be made of just one type and color of flower; I don't mix. It makes more of an impact on a room if the flowers come in dense and profuse bunches, with a fragrance that engulfs you.

Everything else in a room—the furniture, the curtains—is there for the long haul. But flowers embody a moment in time. You enjoy them in each stage from bud to blossom, and then they are gone. The fact that they are ephemeral is part of their beauty. I would never use silk flowers or dried flowers. For me, they're too static and unreal.

PILLOWS Take into account the size of your sofa or chaise, and use a proportionately sized pillow consistently. I prefer to work with larger, standard-size pillows—twenty-four, twenty-six, or twenty-eight inches square. A large

Silk damask pillows lean against suede bolsters, and the contrast of dark and light adds drama to a room. White tulips complement a collection of celadon pottery. Leather welting on these wool pillows adds a subtle detail that relates to the leather sofa, and makes the room feel like an integrated whole.

pillow can anchor a massive piece of upholstery and is also big enough for its own qualities to register. I find postage stamp–size pillows just too cute.

Pillow fabric should be thought of as an integral part of the room's design. It is one more opportunity for layering, according to the principle of yin and yang. If the fabric on the sofa is textured, the pillows could be smooth. If the sofa has a sheen, the pillows could be matte. With a sofa that has many pillows, I usually cover the back row in the same fabric as the sofa, and the pillows in front become the accent.

Pillows are a wonderful way to bring a blast of color or pattern into a neutral room. Since they don't require a lot of yardage, you could splurge on a precious embroidered silk, or find a vintage tapestry fragment that could tie all the colors in the space together. Here is a chance to go for something unexpected, such as turning an old leopard coat into a big sofa pillow. What about cutting up that serape you found on a trip to Mexico, or that Indian sari you stuck in a drawer, or that intricately patterned Japanese obi? I always use hidden zippers so pillow covers can be easily removed for cleaning, or exchanged for a different fabric when you want to shift moods.

HANGING PICTURES Most people hang paintings and photographs too high, which tends to isolate them. In placing art, you have to figure out how to get the greatest mileage out of a piece—how to strategize the placement to help shape the space. If you want to create a sense of intimacy by keeping the eye low in a room, you might hang artworks next to the club chair, or at table height. My rule of thumb is to hang or rest pictures three inches above a table and three inches above a sofa.

Grouping pictures also keeps the art from feeling isolated. When I find a suitable frame, I usually repeat it everywhere. In a large space, I might mix a few different styles of frames, such as bleached wood, mahogany, and gold. I love picture rails, those slim shelves just wide enough to hold a frame. Sometimes I simply prop my photographs against the wall. Then you can move the images around easily, and see them in a different light. When a picture hangs in one place for too long, you stop looking at it.

MY IDEA OF LUXURY

It's the little things that count:

- Wide-plank floorboards.

- Sheet rock covered with four thin layers of joint compound.
  After sanding, the compound will even out the wall.

- Dimmer switches on all lights, and gang switches instead of
  multiple toggles. Whenever it's possible, computerize the lighting.

- Oil-based paints, which are clean, clear, rich, and thick.

- Carpeting that meets the level of surrounding wood and stone floors
  to create a smooth transition.

- Beautiful linens on the bed. It is one of the few places where the
  skin is in direct contact with the house. Like underclothes, it is just for
  you and nobody else. Nice cotton sheets with a high thread count,
  preferably pressed, make you feel pampered.

- Down upholstery.

- Large squares of marble and small grout joints. Tile work in a
  bathroom should run continuously from floor to ceiling.

- Slipcovers on furniture—it gives the room a more throwaway quality.

- A bowl of green apples. A scented candle and incense. Great books
  to browse.

I would like to acknowledge the following people for their support:

To Joseph Montebello, whose idea it was for me to do a book and who made sure it finally got done. Thank you.

To Christine Pittel, who took my disjointed sentences and turned them into sensitive and poetic prose.

To Louis Oliver Gropp for his generous foreword.

To Ann Bramson at Artisan, who believed in this project from the beginning and championed it every step of the way.

To Lisa Yee, who created a beautiful, accessible design, and Nancy Murray, who painstakingly handled the production.

To everyone else at Artisan, thank you for all your help and support.

To the magazines and editors-in-chief for their great encouragement and for helping make my career what it is today:

Paige Rense, *Architectural Digest*;
Margaret Russell, *Elle Decor*;
Dominique Browning, *House & Garden*;
Mark Mayfield, *House Beautiful*;
Cindy Allen, *Interior Design*;
Donna Warner, *Metropolitan Home*;
Pilar Viladas, *The New York Times Magazine*;
and Lisa Newsom, *Veranda*.

To Jane and Richard Novick for their support and trust.

To my wonderful clients and friends without whose endorsement and trust this would not be possible and with special thanks to the clients whose homes appear in the book:

Mr. and Mrs. Steven Arnold, Mr. and Mrs. Harvey Bernstein, Mr. and Mrs. Michael Burke, Dara Caponigro, Monte Coleman, Clive Davis, Susan Dollenmaier, Mr. and Mrs. Raymond Epstein, Chuck Frew, Nely Galan, Mr. and Mrs. Alan Goldberg, Pilar González de Peña, Mr. and Mrs. Michael Lynne, Mark Madoff, Marian McEvoy, Mr. and Mrs. Ronald Ostrow, Mr. and Mrs. Ralph Pucci, Peggy, Mr. and Mrs. Richard Sachs, Mr. and Mrs. Marvin Schur, Shai Tertner, and Mr. and Mrs. Neil Weiss.

To my team for their help with the book:
Laura Cattano, Laura De Peña, Maureen Martin, and David Rogal.

GENERAL STORES
Blackman Cruz
800 North La Cienega Blvd.
Los Angeles, CA 90069
(310) 657-9228
www.blackmancruz.com

Chez Camille
Modern Design
810 North La Cienega Blvd.
Los Angeles, CA 90069
(310) 276-2729
chezcamille@yahoo.com

Therien & Company
411 Vermont St.
San Francisco, CA 94107
(415) 956-8850
www.therien.com

Bosshard Fine Art
Furnishings
112C Camino de la Placita
Taos, NM 87571
(505) 751-9445
www.johnbosshard.com

Range West
815 Dunlap St.
Sante Fe, NM 87501
(505) 986-1568
www.rangewest.com

Ad Hoc
136 Wooster St.
New York, NY 10012
(212) 982-7703
www.adhocny.com

Ralph Pucci International
44 West 18th St.
New York, NY 10011
(212) 633-0452

Sirmos
979 Third Ave.
Suite 1634
New York, NY 10022
(212) 371-0910
www.sirmos.com

Troy
138 Greene St.
New York, NY 10012
(212) 941-4777
www.troysoho.com

VW Home, Inc.
333 West 39th St.
New York, NY 10018
(212) 244-5008
www.vw-home.com

ANTIQUES
Ann Morris Antiques
(including lighting)
239 East 60th St.
New York, NY 10022
(212) 755-3170

H.M. Luther, Inc.
61 East 11th St.
New York, NY 10003
(212) 505-1485

Jacques Carcanagues, Inc.
21 Greene St.
New York, NY 10012
(212) 925-8110
carcan@rcn.com

Lou Marotta (NY), Inc.
243 East 60th St.
New York, NY 10022
(212) 223-0306
www.loumarotta.com

Maison Gerard Ltd.
53 East 10th St.
New York, NY 10003
(212) 674-7611
www.maisongerard.com

Tucker Robbins Unlimited
33-02 Skillman Ave.
4th Floor
Long Island City, NY 11101
(212) 366-4427
www.tuckerrobbins.com

ART GALLERIES
Howard Greenberg Gallery
120 Wooster St.
2nd Floor
New York, NY 10012
(212) 334-0010
www.howardgreenberg.com

Janet Borden, Inc.
560 Broadway
New York, NY 10012
(212) 431-0166
www.janetbordeninc.com

Robert Miller Gallery
524 West 26th St.
New York, NY 10001
(212) 366-4774
www.robertmillergallery.com

AUDIO VISUAL
Electronic Environments Ltd.
247 West 37th St.
Suite 704
New York, NY 10018
(212) 997-1110

BATHROOM & KITCHEN
Waterworks
(800) 899-6757
www.waterworks.com

BEDDING
Charles H. Beckley, Inc.
979 Third Ave.
Suite 911
New York, NY 10022
(212) 759-8450
www.chbeckley.com

ELECTRICAL LAMP MOUNTINGS
Joseph Richter, Inc.
249 East 57th St.
New York, NY 10022
(212) 755-6094
www.josephrichterinc.com

FIREPLACE SURROUNDS
Danny Alessandro Ltd.
308 East 59th St.
New York, NY 10022
(212) 759-8210
www.alessandroltd.com

FLOORING (CARPETS)
Doris Leslie Blau Ltd.
(antique carpets)
724 Fifth Ave.
6th Floor
New York, NY 10019
(212) 586-5511
www.dorisleslieblau.com

Stark Carpet Corp.
979 Third Ave.
11th Floor
New York, NY 10022
(212) 752-9000
www.starkcarpet.com

Tufenkian Tibetan Carpets
(contemporary carpets)
902 Broadway
2nd Floor
New York, NY 10010
(212) 475-2475
www.tufenkiancarpets.com

FLORISTS
Preston Bailey Design, Inc.
147 West 25th St.
11th Floor
New York, NY 10001
(212) 691-6777

Zezé Flowers
398 East 52nd St.
New York, NY 10022
(212) 753-7767

FRAMEMAKERS
A.P.F. Master Framemakers
172 East 75th St.
New York, NY 10021
(212) 988-1090

GLASS & MIRRORS
Galaxy
277 Fairfield Rd.
Fairfield, NJ 07004
(973) 575-3440
(800) 378-9042
www.galaxycustom.com

Jesse Shapiro &
James Glass Corp.
445 Gerard Ave.
Bronx, NY 10451
(718) 292-3000

HARDWARE
Nanz Custom Hardware
20 Van Dam St.
New York, NY 10013
(212) 367-7000
www.nanz.com

P.E. Guerin, Inc.
23 Jane St.
New York, NY 10014
(212) 243-5270
www.peguerin.com

Simon's Hardware & Bath
421 Third Ave.
New York, NY 10016
(212) 532-9220
(888) 274-6667

LAMPSHADES
Shades from
the Midnight Sun
66 Boulder Trail
Bronxville, NY 10708
(914) 779-7237

LEATHER
Teddy & Arthur Edelman Ltd.
979 Third Ave.
Suite 214
New York, NY 10022
(212) 751-3339
www.edelmanleather.com

LIGHTING
David Weeks
Lighting Studio
61 Pearl St.
Brooklyn, NY 11201
(718) 596-7945
www.davidweekslighting.com
www.davidweeksstudio.com

Hinson & Company
979 Third Ave.
7th Floor
New York, NY 10022
(212) 688-5538

Lee's Studio Lighting
1069 Third Ave.
New York, NY 10021
(212) 371-1122
www.leesstudio.com

MSK Illuminations, Inc.
235 East 57th St.
New York, NY 10022
(212) 888-6474
www.mskillumination.com

LINENS
Anichini New York
230 Fifth Ave.
Suite 1900
New York, NY 10018
(800) 522-8639
www.anichini.com

MARBLE
Vernon Marble
and Granite, Inc.
37-21 Vernon Blvd.
Long Island City, NY 11101
(718) 472-1500

PAINT
Benjamin Moore & Co.
51 Chestnut Ridge Rd.
Montvale, NJ 07645
(800) 344-0400
www.benjaminmoore.com

PAINT FINISHES
Douglas Wilson Ltd.
336 West 37th St.
Suite 3SE
New York, NY 10018
(212) 594-7365
www.douglaswilson.ws

SPECIAL EVENTS PLANNERS
Shiraz NYC
347 West 39th St.
New York, NY 10018
(212) 643-2483
www.shiraznyc.com

TABLE BASES
West Coast Industries, Inc.
707 East 7th St.
Los Angeles, CA 90021
(800) 243-7707
www.westcoastindustries.com

AFRICA
Amatuli Fine Art C.C.
Postnet Suite 45
Private Bag
South Africa 1685
011.27.11.440.5065
amatuli@global.co.za

BELGIUM
G.A. Aquarius
23 rue Watteeu
Brussels 1000
011.322.511.45.72

Galerie Yannick David
23 rue Watteeu
Brussels 1000
011.322.513.37.48
yannick.david.antiques@skynet.be

Robert Zurcher
59 bis rue des Minimes
Brussels 1000
011.322.502.53.04

DENMARK
Ellekilde Auktionshus A/S
Bredgade 25
1260 Copenhagen
011.45.33.91.11.21
www.ellekilde.dk

ENGLAND
Francesca Martire
Stand f.131-137
1st Floor
13-25 Alfie's Market
Church St.
London NW8 ORH
011.44.71.723.1370

Guinevere Antiques Ltd.
574-580 Kings Rd.
London SW6 2DY
011.44.20.7736.2917

M.J. Black
Stand 666/8
Alfie's Market
13-25 Church St.
London NW8 8DT
011.44.71.723.0678

FRANCE
Alain Lagrange
Stand 227, Allée #4
Marché Paul-Bert
St. Ouen 93400
011.33.6.15.23.89.18

Anne Jaudel Antiquités
5 rue de l'Université
Paris 75007
011.33.1.42.60.33.94

Corinne et Gérard Mahé
Stand 31, Allée #1
Marché Serpette
110 rue des Rosiers
St. Ouen 93400
011.33.1.40.12.81.22

Galerie L
54 rue Jacob
Paris 75006
011.33.1.42.86.07.55

Galerie Nicole Mugler
2 rue de l'Université
Paris 75007
011.33.1.42.96.36.45

Lucien Pineau
Stand 4, Allée #5
Marché Serpette
St. Ouen 93400
011.31.1.40.11.45.75

HONG KONG
China Curios Centre
12 Upper Lascar Row
Sheung Wan
011.852.2543.1006

Chine Gallery
No. 42A, Hollywood Rd.
Sheung Wan
011.852.2543.0023
www.chinegallery.com

Martin Fung Antiques
148 Hollywood Rd.
Sheung Wan
011.852.2549.2361

Willow Gallery Ltd
159-163 Hollywood Rd.
Shop D
Sheung Wan
011.852.2544.0996
www.wgintltd@netvigator.com

INDIA
Amrapali Jewels Pvt. Ltd
Panch Batti, M.I. Rd.
Jaipur 302001
011.91.141.377940

Central Cottage
Industries Emporium
Jawaharvyaparbhawan
Janpath, New Delhi 110001
011.91.11.3326790

Manglam Arts
Govind Nagar
Amber Palace Rd.
Jaipur 302002
011.91.11.553614
manglam@jp1.dot.net.in

ITALY
Antichità Gabriele
Troncone
Via Foria, 262
Napoli 80137
011.39.81.451513

Apollonia Antichità
Via Rosselli, 26/a
(S.S. Adriatica)
Via Cavour
(vic. Giardino d'Estate)
Porto San Giorgio (AP) 63017
011.39.734.676877
www.appollonia.com

Fauro Antichità
Via Monserrato, 120
Roma 00186
011.39.6.6867747

The Hobby Horse
1826, Frezzeria, L. Marco
Venezia 30100
011.39.41.5226050

La Torre di Lovato
Andrea & Co.
Via Ponte Pietra, 29/B
Verona 37121
011.39.45.8000344

Le Arti Decorative
Via XX Marzo 11
(vic. Leon d'Oro, 4)
Parma 43100
011.39.521.234353

Marcello Raspante
Antichità
Via Nicolo Garzilli, 39/A
Palermo 90100
011.39.91.6112899

NETHERLANDS
Pol's Potten
hornweg 77a
1432 GD Aalsmeer
011.31.297.329222
www.polspotten.nl

SRI LANKA
Prema Brothers
No. 757 Peraileniya Rd.
Kandy (Ceylon)
011.94.8.232695

Villa Saffron
411, Sri Jayawardenapura
Mawatha
Welikada, Rajagiriya
011.94.1.75.331651

SWEDEN
Artique Konst &
Antikhandel
Grev Turegatan 46
Stockholm 11438
011.46.8.660.51.22

Bukowskis
Arsenalsgatan 4
Stockholm 11187
011.46.8.614.08.00

THAILAND
Ashwood Gallery
River City
Shopping Complex
Suites 314 & 430
23 Yotha Rd.
Sampanthawong
Bangkok 10100
011.662.237.0077 ex31

Asian Galleries
River City
Shopping Complex
Suites 342 & 343
23 Yotha Rd.
Sampanthawong
Bangkok 10100
011.662.237.0077

Asian Primitive
River City
Shopping Complex
Suite 333
23 Yotha Rd.
Sampanthawong
Bangkok 10100
011.662.237.0077.8 EXT. 333

Jiraporn Art & Antiques
River City
Shopping Complex
Suite 446
23 Yotha Rd.
Sampanthawong
Bangkok 10100
011.662.237.0077 EXT. 446

Panne
River City
Shopping Complex
Suite 252
23 Yotha Rd.
Sampanthawong
Bangkok 10100

Robert McLeod–
Ancient Pottery
43/11 Sukhumvit 11
Bangkok 10110
011.662.250.1323